New Directions for
Adult and Continuing
Education

Susan Imel
Jovita M. Ross-Gordon
COEDITORS-IN-CHIEF

Third Update on Adult Learning Theory

Sharan B. Merriam

EDITOR

Number 119 • Fall 2008
Jossey-Bass
San Francisco

THIRD UPDATE ON ADULT LEARNING THEORY
Sharan B. Merriam (ed.)
New Directions for Adult and Continuing Education, no. 119
Susan Imel, Jovita M. Ross-Gordon, Coeditors-in-Chief

Microfilm copies of issues and articles are available in 16mm and 35mm, as well as microfiche in 105mm, through University Microfilms Inc., 300 North Zeeb Road, Ann Arbor, Michigan 48106-1346.

NEW DIRECTIONS FOR ADULT AND CONTINUING EDUCATION (ISSN 1052-2891, electronic ISSN 1536-0717) is part of The Jossey-Bass Higher and Adult Education Series and is published quarterly by Wiley Subscription Services, Inc., A Wiley Company, at Jossey-Bass, 989 Market Street, San Francisco, California 94103-1741. Periodicals Postage Paid at San Francisco, California, and at additional mailing offices. POSTMASTER: Send address changes to New Directions for Adult and Continuing Education, Jossey-Bass, 989 Market Street, San Francisco, California 94103-1741.

New Directions for Adult and Continuing Education is indexed in CIJE: Current Index to Journals in Education (ERIC); Contents Pages in Education (T&F); ERIC Database (Education Resources Information Center; Higher Education Abstracts (Claremont Graduate University); and Sociological Abstracts (CSA/CIG).

SUBSCRIPTIONS cost $89.00 for individuals and $228.00 for institutions, agencies, and libraries.

EDITORIAL CORRESPONDENCE should be sent to the Coeditors-in-Chief, Susan Imel, ERIC/ACVE, 1900 Kenny Road, Columbus, Ohio 43210-1090, e-mail: imel.l@osu.edu; or Jovita M. Ross-Gordon, Southwest Texas State University, EAPS Dept., 601 University Drive, San Marcos, TX 78666.

Cover photograph by Jack Hollingsworth@Photodisc

www.josseybass.com

CONTENTS

EDITOR'S NOTES

Adult learning is at the heart of all adult education practice. From adult basic education to continuing professional education, from the workplace to an art museum, from a community college to a Bible study class, enabling the learning of adults is the glue that holds us together. The more we know about how adults learn, the more effective we can be in our work as adult educators.

It is thus the intent of this volume, *The Third Update on Adult Learning Theory,* to update readers on new thinking and research in adult learning.

This sourcebook follows two previous editions on the same topic, the first published in 1993 and the second in 2001. Both editions have been very popular, here and overseas, especially as companion books in adult learning courses. The value of these sourcebooks, including this third edition, is to bring together in one volume some of the latest thinking on adult learning. Readers do not have to search myriad research journals to find out what's new; the authors of each chapter have done that for us! At the same time, the updates are not designed for comprehensive coverage of all that we know about adult learning; rather, they offer glimpses of new thinking about adult learning, glimpses that may or may not develop into more comprehensive models or theories of adult learning.

A quick review of the two previous updates reveals how quickly things are changing. The 1993 sourcebook included chapters on andragogy, self-directed learning, transformational learning, critical theory, and feminist pedagogy. Although certainly andragogy and self-directed learning were not new, the chapter authors sought to update the research in these two areas. Transformational learning was also not new in the sense that Mezirow began publishing articles on the topic years earlier, followed by a book in 1990. However, there was no single place where his ideas were brought together until the chapter in the 1993 update.

In the 2001 update, andragogy and self-directed learning were reviewed in a single chapter as two foundational pillars of adult learning theory. The chapter on transformative learning was retained because it wasn't until the 1990s that actual empirical, data-based research began appearing along with a few alternative frameworks to Mezirow's theory. A chapter in 1993 on situated cognition became a chapter on context-based learning in 2001. Likewise, a chapter on consciousness and learning in 1993 became The Brain and Consciousness in 2001. The new chapters in 2001 were on emotions and learning, informal and incidental learning, and critical and postmodern perspectives and somatic and narrative learning.

NEW DIRECTIONS FOR ADULT AND CONTINUING EDUCATION, no. 119, Fall 2008 © 2008 Wiley Periodicals, Inc.
Published online in Wiley InterScience (www.interscience.wiley.com) • DOI: 10.1002/ace.300

When I was invited to consider putting together a *Third Update on Adult Learning Theory,* I had to first ask myself and other colleagues what indeed was new; what was on the horizon that would warrant another volume? This thinking was also informed by having completed a third edition of *Learning in Adulthood* with colleagues Rosemary Caffarella and Lisa Baumgartner. From this experience and from discussions with colleagues, the topics for this third update were determined.

Transformative learning theory, although not a new topic, was retained in this update because the amount of research and writing has substantially increased since the 2001 sourcebook. As an indicator of this burgeoning interest in transformative learning, there have been seven international conferences devoted to this topic, the most recent being in October 2007. Ed Taylor first reviews the main tenets of transformative learning theory according to its main architect, Jack Mezirow. Taylor then describes a number of alternative conceptions of transformative learning, the most recent being neurobiological, cultural-spiritual, race-centric, and planetary views. He then discusses what these new insights into transformative learning have to say with regard to the practice of fostering such learning.

The second chapter in this update reflects recent shifts in thinking about learning in the workplace. Historically, learning in the workplace has been construed as training; many organizations had (and still have) training departments with training directors. Tara Fenwick points out that a focus on learning in the workplace is a much more accurate assessment of what actually takes place. Educators in the workplace are trying to figure out how people solve workplace problems through learning, and how particular groups of workers learn. She posits that these two concerns have brought about a shift in conceptions of workplace learning.

Perhaps more than other adult learning topics, the popular press has brought spirituality forward, especially as it manifests in the workplace and higher education. In the third chapter of this volume, Libby Tisdell—who herself has done substantial research on spirituality in adult education— explores the notion of spirituality through looking at a definition, its relationship to adult development, and how we can create space for it in our adult education classes.

Another new area for adult learning, and one that was presented only briefly in the 2001 update, is that of embodied or somatic knowing. It has always been a part of our learning, but the Western focus on cognitive processing has ignored the body as a site of learning. In Chapter Four, Tammy Freiler refers to the growing research base on this topic and explores how one can learn through the body. Embodied learning is an alternate way of knowing that reconnects the mind and body.

This connection between the mind and body is actually reinforced in Kathleen Taylor and Annalee Lamoreaux's chapter on the latest developments in the neuroscience of learning. They first explain how the brain works, the complexity of the brain, and then how learning, embodied experience, and reflection interact in making meaningful connections in the brain. Brain imaging techniques have revealed how learning changes the brain itself. The authors also suggest how adult educators might maximize learning through knowing how the brain "develops."

The next chapter, on narrative learning, by Carolyn Clark and Marsha Rossiter, brings to our attention how stories connect with learning. As with embodied learning, narrative learning was only briefly mentioned in the 2001 update. A recent book by these authors as well as a growing research base have moved narrative learning from the margins of adult learning theory to a more central position. As they point out, human beings have always told stories to make sense of the world and convey "truths" of the culture. What is new is how stories are a form of meaning making or learning. We learn through stories, and creating a narrative to make sense of our experience is itself learning.

Chapter Seven, by Young Sek Kim and me, introduces readers to non-Western conceptions of learning and knowing. Whether one studies indigenous knowledge systems of indigenous peoples in the West and across the globe or religious and philosophically based systems such as Confucianism, Buddhism, or Islam, there are commonalities that can inform adult learning theory. Learning is a holistic activity involving the mind, body, and spirit. It is also a collective activity in that learning is done with the community for the benefit of the community. In these systems, learning is also truly lifelong.

In Chapter Eight, Bob Hill takes us to the edges of postmodernism, asserting that we are in a new New Social Movement called the Convergence Movement. Learning in this "moment" means being increasingly skeptical about universal truths, or metanarratives. He sees the Convergence Movement as critiquing "the intersection of adult learning and social justice from a postmodern frame." Hill maintains that the Convergence Movement, unlike postmodernism, offers more than critique; it poses creative solutions to oppression and marginalization. Meaning making is the imaginative employment of for example, humor, street theater, dance, and song.

In the final chapter in this volume, I review the previous eight chapters and make some observations as to how adult learning theory appears to be developing. First, there is growing attention to the contexts where learning takes place and how those contexts shape learning. Second, and quite clearly, adult learning is no longer focused on the individual's cognitive processing. Adult learning is much more of a multidimensional, holistic phenomenon where the body, the emotions, and the spirit count as much as the intellect. This enlarged conception of adult learning has also engendered attention to more creative and artistic approaches in practice.

I would like to personally thank each and every author who so professionally responded to the invitation to contribute to this volume. To a person, you were wonderful to work with. I'd also like to thank Jovita Ross-Gordon and Susan Imel, editors of the New Directions for Adult and Continuing Education series, for their helpful suggestions and guidance in this process.

Sharan B. Merriam
Editor

SHARAN B. MERRIAM is professor of adult education at the University of Georgia, Athens.

New Directions for Adult and Continuing Education • DOI: 10.1002/ace

1

This chapter updates transformative learning theory through discussing emerging alternative theoretical conceptions, current research findings, and implications for practice.

Transformative Learning Theory

Edward W. Taylor

There is an instinctive drive among all humans to make meaning of their daily lives. Because there are no enduring truths, and change is continuous, we cannot always be assured of what we know or believe. It therefore becomes imperative in adulthood that we develop a more critical worldview as we seek ways to better understand our world. This involves learning "how to negotiate and act upon our own purposes, values, feelings and meanings rather than those we have uncritically assimilated from others" (Mezirow and Associates, p. 2000, p. 8). Developing more reliable beliefs, exploring and validating their fidelity, and making informed decisions are fundamental to the adult learning process. It is transformative learning theory that explains this learning process of constructing and appropriating new and revised interpretations of the meaning of an experience in the world.

Thirty years ago, when Jack Mezirow (1978) first introduced a theory of adult learning, it helped explain how adults changed the way they interpreted their world. This theory of transformative learning is considered uniquely adult—that is, grounded in human communication, where "learning is understood as the process of using a prior interpretation to construe a new or revised interpretation of the meaning of one's experience in order to guide future action" (Mezirow, 1996, p. 162). The transformative process is formed and circumscribed by a frame of reference. Frames of reference are structures of assumptions and expectations that frame an individual's tacit points of view and influence their thinking, beliefs, and actions. It is the revision of a frame of reference in concert with reflection on experience that is addressed by the theory of perspective transformation—a paradigmatic shift. A perspective transformation leads to "a more fully developed (more functional) frame of

NEW DIRECTIONS FOR ADULT AND CONTINUING EDUCATION, no. 119, Fall 2008 © 2008 Wiley Periodicals, Inc.
Published online in Wiley InterScience (www.interscience.wiley.com) • DOI: 10.1002/ace.301

reference . . . one that is more (a) inclusive, (b) differentiating, (c) permeable, (d) critically reflective, and (e) integrative of experience" (Mezirow, 1996, p. 163). A perspective transformation often occurs either through a series of cumulative transformed meaning schemes or as a result of an acute personal or social crisis, for example, a natural disaster, the death of a significant other, divorce, a debilitating accident, war, job loss, or retirement. These experiences are often stressful and painful, and they can cause individuals to question the very core of their existence (Mezirow, 1997). An example of a perspective transformation is illustrated by Marie Claire, an American, who describes her experience of moving to Switzerland for a number of years:

> I was very sheltered before [moving]. I think it made me aware of the fact that there are people who do things differently. There are different cultures. . . . I tended to look at things a lot more basic. . . . People are the same all over the world to a certain extent. You got to go to work. You got to do your daily job. I tended not to be so narrow minded. . . . What I really thought about the United States was how shallow, how provincial. . . . We didn't know anything about other countries, we were so isolated. We always thought we were the best. I was starting to think that maybe we weren't the best, because we are missing out on so much. When you're living in Europe you're exposed to so many different languages and cultures and so much history and beauty that we miss out on here. We are isolated, so I started to think of my country as not being number one anymore [Taylor, 1993, p. 179].

Central to Marie Claire's transformation is her intercultural experience, critical reflecting on her experience, and engaging in dialogue with others. Her experience of learning to adjust to living in Switzerland becomes the gist for critical reflection: "[Shared] learning experiences establish a common base from which each learner constructs meaning through personal reflection and group discussion. . . . The meanings that learners attach to their experiences may be subjected to critical scrutiny" (Tennant, 1991, p. 197). Critical scrutiny, or more specifically critical reflection, is seen as conscious and explicit reassessment of the consequence and origin of our meaning structures. It "is a process by which we attempt to justify our beliefs, either by rationally examining assumptions, often in response to intuitively becoming aware that something is wrong with the result of our thought, or challenging its validity through discourse with others of differing viewpoints and arriving at the best informed judgment" (Mezirow, 1995, p. 46).

Marie Claire's discourse with others in the host culture was the medium through which transformation was promoted and developed. However, in contrast to everyday discussions, this kind of discourse is used "when we have reason to question the comprehensibility, truth, appropriateness (in relation to norms), or authenticity (in relation to feelings) of what is being asserted" (Mezirow, 1991, p. 77). Through multiple interactions with others, Marie Claire questioned her deeply held assumptions about her own culture in relationship to the host culture.

Since the early 1980s, this learning theory has spawned a number of alternative theoretical conceptions and a treasure chest of research about both the basic assumptions of transformative learning and the fostering of transformative learning in the classroom. The next section discusses emerging conceptions of transformative learning, followed by related research on the practice of transformative learning.

Alternative Conceptions of Transformative Learning

The ubiquitous acceptance of Mezirow's psychocritical view of transformative learning theory has often led to an uncontested assumption that there is a singular conception of transformative learning, overshadowing a growing presence of other theoretical conceptions. Even though efforts have been made in the past to make sense of varied perspectives (for example, Dirkx, 1998; Taylor, 1998), their numbers were limited and contributions to transformative learning not fully appreciated. At present, it can be argued that there are a variety of alternative conceptions of transformative learning theory that refer to similar ideas and address factors often overlooked in the dominant theory of transformation (Mezirow's), such as the role of spirituality, positionality, emancipatory learning, and neurobiology. The exciting part of this diversity of theoretical perspectives is that it has the potential to offer a more diverse interpretation of transformative learning and have significant implications for practice.

To bring the reader up to date, in the previous edition of this volume (Merriam, 2001), there were three alternative perspectives discussed in contrast to Mezirow's psychocritical perspective of transformative learning: psychoanalytic, psychodevelopmental, and social emancipatory. A *psychoanalytic* view of transformative learning is seen as a process of individuation, a lifelong journey of coming to understand oneself through reflecting on the psychic structures (ego, shadow, persona, collective unconscious, and so on) that make up an individual's identity. Individuation involves discovery of new talents, a sense of empowerment and confidence, a deeper understanding of one's inner self, and a greater sense of self-responsibility (Boyd and Meyers, 1988; Cranton, 2000; Dirkx, 2000). A *psychodevelopmental* view of transformative learning is a view across the lifespan, reflecting continuous, incremental, and progressive growth. Central to this view of transformation is epistemological change (change in how we make meaning), not just change in behavioral repertoire or quantity of knowledge. In addition, there is appreciation for the role of relationships, personal contextual influences, and holistic ways of knowing in transformative learning, that have been often overlooked in Mezirow's rational emphasis on transformation (Daloz, 1986; Kegan, 1994).

In the latter two perspectives, including Mezirow's psychocritical view, the unit of analysis is the individual, with little consideration given to the role of context and social change in the transformative experience.

New Directions for Adult and Continuing Education • DOI: 10.1002/ace

On the other hand, a third alternative perspective, a *social-emancipatory* view, in a small way starts to address these concerns. Rooted primarily in the work of Freire (1984), this perspective is about developing an "onto-logical vocation" (p. 12), a theory of existence that views people as subjects, not objects, who are constantly reflecting and acting on the transformation of their world so it can become a more equitable place for all to live. Its goal is social transformation by demythicizing reality, where the oppressed develop a critical consciousness (that is, conscientization).

Three teaching approaches are central to fostering emancipatory trans-formative learning (Freire and Macedo, 1995). First is the centrality of crit-ical reflection, with the purpose of rediscovering power and helping learners develop an awareness of agency to transform society and their own reality. Second, a liberating approach to teaching couched in "acts of cognition not in the transferal of information" (p. 67) is a "problem-posing" (p. 70) and dialogical methodology. Third is a horizontal student-teacher relationship where the teacher works as a political agent and on an equal footing with students.

In addition to the previously discussed views, four additional views of transformative learning (neurobiological, cultural-spiritual, race-centric, planetary) have lately emerged in the field. Most recent is the *neurobiologi-cal* perspective of transformative learning (Janik, 2005). This "brain-based" theory was discovered by clinicians using medical imaging techniques to study brain functions of patients who were recovering from psychological trauma. What these researchers determined was that a neurobiological transformation is seen as invoking "the parasympathetic branch of the auto-nomic nervous system, and the hypothalamic-pituitary pitocin secreting endocrine system to alter learning during periods of search and discovery" (Janik, 2007, p. 12). In simpler terms, the findings suggest that the brain structure actually changes during the learning process. These findings in turn bring into question traditional models of learning (behaviorism, cog-nitivism, constructivism) and instead offer a distinctive neurobiological, physically based pathway to transformative learning. From this perspective, learning is seen as "volitional, curiosity-based, discovery-driven, and mentor-assisted" and most effective at higher cognitive levels (Janik, 2005, p. 144). Furthermore, a neurobiological approach suggests that transformative learning (1) requires discomfort prior to discovery; (2) is rooted in students' experiences, needs, and interests; (3) is strengthened by emotive, sensory, and kinesthetic experiences; (4) appreciates differences in learning between males and females, and (5) demands that educators acquire an understanding of a unique discourse and knowledge base of neurobiological systems.

A *cultural-spiritual* view of transformative learning (see Brooks, 2000; Tisdell, 2003) is concerned with the "connections between individuals and social structures . . . and notions of intersecting positionalities" (Tisdell, 2005, p. 256). This perspective focuses on how learners construct knowledge (narratives) as part of the transformative learning experience. In particular, it appreciates a culturally relevant and spiritually grounded approach to transformative pedagogy. Its goal is to foster a narrative transformation—engaging storytelling on a personal and social level through group inquiry. Cross-cultural relationships are also encouraged, along with developing spiritual awareness. The teacher's role is that of a collaborator with a relational emphasis on group inquiry and narrative reasoning, which assist the learner in sharing stories of experience and revising new stories in the process.

A *race-centric* view of transformative learning puts people of African descent, most often black women, at the center, where they are the subjects of the transformative experience. As a non-Eurocentric orientation of transformative learning (Williams, 2003), it is in the early stages of theoretical development where race is the predominant unit of analysis with an emphasis on the social-political dimensions of learning. Like Freire's emancipatory perspective, the vocabulary associated with transformative learning is often not used: "Traditionally, African people have had systems of education that were transformative. Rites of passage and rituals are among the many forms Africans have created to nurture the consciousness of every member of society into a greater connection with the Self, the Community, and the Universe " (p. 463). It is a conception of transformative learning that is culturally bounded, oppositional, and nonindividualistic. Essential to this view is engaging the polyrhythmic realities—"the students' lived experience within a sociocultural, political, and historical context" (Sheared, 1994, p. 36). In addition, there are three key concepts in fostering transformative learning: promoting inclusion (giving voice to the historically silenced), promoting empowerment (not self-actualization but belongingness and equity as a cultural member), and learning to negotiate effectively between and across cultures. Fostering transformative learning is seen as a deliberate and conscious strategy in employing a political framework (consciousness raising, activism, fostering a safe learning environment) with the expectation that it "may be necessary for one to undergo some form of self-reflection and transformation in order to teach transformation" (Johnson-Bailey and Alfred, 2006, p. 55). This conception of transformative learning has the potential to address some of the concerns raised by Brookfield (2003) by foregrounding the interest of black students, instead of as the "other" or as an alternative view.

A *planetary* view of transformative learning takes in the totality of life's context beyond the individual and addresses fundamental issues in the field of education as a whole (O'Sullivan, 1999). The goal of transformative education from this perspective is reorganization of the whole system (political, social, educational). It is creating a new story from one that is dysfunctional and rooted in technical-industrial values of Western Eurocentric culture, which gives little appreciation to the natural, or to an integral worldview. This view recognizes the interconnectedness among universe, planet, natural environment, human community, and personal world. Most significant is recognizing the individual not just from a social-political dimension but also from an ecological and planetary one. Transformation is not only about how we view our human counterparts; it explores how we, as humans, relate with the physical world.

Key differences exist among the various views of transformative learning. Beginning with the goal of transformation, one of the most fundamental differences is that of personal or emancipatory transformation (self-actualization to planetary consciousness). Related to this difference is the emphasis on individual or social change. Those views that are more rooted in the individual (psychocritical, psychoanalytic, psychodevelopmental, neurobiological) give little attention to context and social change and their relationship to transformation. Where the individual and society are seen as one and the same (emancipatory, race-centric, cultural-spiritual), transformative learning is as much about social change as individual transformation. Another difference is the role of culture in transformative learning. The more psychologically centered models (psychoanalytic, psychodevelopmental, psychocritical, neurobiological) tend to reflect a more universal view of learning, with little appreciation for the role of social or cultural differences. On the other hand, those views that recognize difference (social emancipatory, culturally relevant narrative, race-centric, and planetary) place much greater emphasis on positionality (where one's "position" is relative to race, class, gender, sexual orientation) and its relationship to both the process and the practice of transformative learning.

New Insights from Research and Implications for Practice

Along with emerging alternative perspectives on transformative learning theory, research continues to flourish as to the nature of transformative learning. In my recent critical review of research (Taylor, 2007), a number of findings have implications as to the process of transformative learning and how it can be fostered in the classroom. Even though most research continues to be situated in higher education settings, the focus has shifted somewhat away from the possibility of a transformation in relationship to a particular life event, toward greater interest in factors that shape the transformative experience (critical reflection, holistic approaches, and relationships).

To begin with the construct "perspective transformation," as previously discussed, it has been found to be an enduring and irreversible process (Courtenay, Merriam, and Reeves, 1998). In addition, research further substantiates the relationship between action and perspective transformation (MacLeod, Parkin, Pullon, and Robertson, 2003). For example, Lange (2004) found a transformation in fostering citizen action toward a sustainable society to be more than an epistemological change in worldview; it also involved an ontological shift, reflective of a need to act on the new perspective. These studies along with others suggest that it is important for educators to create opportunities for learners within and outside the class-room to act on new insights in the process of transformative learning. Without experiences to test and explore new perspectives, it is unlikely learners will fully transform.

Second, there are new insights about critical reflection and its significance to transformative learning. In particular, they shed light on the nature of reflection, factors that influence reflection, indicators of reflection, joint reflection through peer dialogue, and factors that help explain nonreflection. For example, recognizing levels of reflection using categories developed by Mezirow (content, process, premise), Kreber (2004) concluded that when learning, in this case about teaching, teachers may need at times to begin with premise reflection—that is, being more concerned with *why* they teach than with how or what they teach. Premise reflection involves critically "questioning our presuppositions underlying our knowledge" (p. 31).

In addition, critical reflection seems to be a developmental process, rooted in experience. It begins to give credence to Merriam's position (2004) that "mature cognitive development is foundational to engaging in critical reflection and rational discourse necessary for transformative learning" (p. 65). For educators, these findings suggest the importance of engaging learners in classroom practices that assist in the development of critical reflection through use of reflective journaling, classroom dialogue, and critical questioning. Furthermore, it also means recognizing that becoming more reflective is a developmental process requiring time and continuous practice.

Third, research further substantiates the importance of a holistic approach to transformative learning in addition to the often-emphasized use of rational discourse and critical reflection. A holistic approach recognizes the role of feelings, other ways of knowing (intuition, somatic), and the role of relationships with others in the process of transformative learning. Dirkx (2006) suggests it is "about inviting 'the whole person' into the classroom environment, we mean the person in fullness of being: as an affective, intuitive, thinking, physical, spiritual self" (p. 46). By engaging the affective, it provides "an opportunity, for establishing a dialogue with those unconscious aspects of ourselves seeking expression through various images, feelings, and behaviors within the learning setting" (Dirkx, 2006, p. 22). For practitioners this means actively dialoguing about the feelings of learners, in concert with reason, when fostering transformative learning.

Other holistic approaches include the importance of relationships with others in fostering transformative learning. Types of relationship found to be most significant for transformation are love relationships (enhanced self-image, friendship), memory relationships (former or deceased individuals), and imaginative relationships (inner-dialogue, meditation; Carter, 2002). In addition to the typologies of relationships Eisen (2001) identified a "peer dynamic" among successful peer-learning partnerships on the part of community college teachers. This dynamic reflected a number of essential relational qualities: nonhierarchical status, nonevaluative feedback, voluntary participation, partner selection, authenticity, and establishment of mutual goals.

Fourth, there has been an interest in the lack of transformation among some individuals and barriers that discourage and inhibit transformation. The lack of change seems to be explained by a variety of factors. For example, in a study that explored how learners made meaning of their life histories via dialogue in an online graduate course on adult development, researchers found a lack of critical reflection among learners because "group members did not ask critical questions of one another or challenge each other's assumptions. This lack of critique may have truncated the group process prematurely" (Ziegler, Paulus, and Woodside, 2006, p. 315). Another explanation for nonreflective learning is shown through learning preferences in the use of reflective journaling (Chimera, 2006). Some learners who were classified as nonreflectors when their journals were analyzed were found to prefer talking about issues rather than writing them in a journal. Some did not see it as necessary to write their thoughts down and therefore did not see a need for journal writing. This lack of change on the individual level should remind educators that it is important to take time to know students as individuals, recognizing their preferences, and engaging a variety of approaches in fostering transformative learning.

Identifying barriers that inhibit transformative learning can also help explain a lack of change among students. Examples of barriers are rules and sanctions imposed on welfare women returning to work in a family empowerment project (Christopher, Dunnagan, Duncan, and Paul, 2001); the downside of cohort experiences, where there is often an unequal distribution of group responsibilities and emphasis on task completion instead of reflective dialogue (Scribner and Donaldson, 2001); and rigid role assignments (Taylor, 2003).

A response to learner resistance and barriers to transformative learning is for educators to develop awareness of learner readiness for change. Recent research reveals that it is important to appreciate the role of life experience among learners and become more aware of learners who are susceptible to or who desire change. For example, life experience has been found to be particularly significant in online settings (Cragg, Plotnikoff, Hugo, and Casey, 2001; Ziegahn, 2001). Greater life experience seems to constitute a "deeper well" from which to draw and react to discussion that emerged among online participants.

Final Thoughts

Transformative learning theory continues to be a growing area of study of adult learning and has significant implications for the practice of teaching adults. The growth is so significant that it seems to have replaced andragogy as the dominant educational philosophy of adult education, offering teaching practices grounded in empirical research and supported by sound theoretical assumptions. Also, as previously discussed, there is the emerging presence of alternative conceptions of transformative learning, challenging scholars and educators to look beyond transformative learning as defined by Mezirow. These alternative perspectives offer fresh insights and encourage greater research in the area of transformative learning.

Despite the growth in understanding transformative learning, there is still much not known about the practice of transformative learning in the classroom. One area in particular is the student's role in fostering transformative learning. What are the student's responsibilities in relationship to the transformative educator? Second, there is a need to understand the peripheral consequences of fostering transformative learning in the classroom. For example, how does a student's transformation affect peers in the classroom, the teacher, the educational institution, and other individuals who play a significant role in the life of the student? Furthermore, there is little known about the impact of fostering transformative learning on learner outcomes (grades, test scores). Definitive support is needed if educators are going to recognize fostering transformative learning as a worthwhile teaching approach with adult learners.

Finally, the growing body of research and alternative perspectives should remind educators that fostering transformative learning is much more than implementing a series of instructional strategies with adult learners. Transformative learning is first and foremost about educating from a particular worldview, a particular educational philosophy. It is also not an easy way to teach. Wearing the title, or moniker, of a transformative educator "should not be taken lightly or without considerable personal reflection. Although the rewards may be great for both the teacher and the learner, it demands a great deal of work, skill, and courage" (Taylor, 2006, p. 92). It means asking yourself, Am I willing to transform in the process of helping my students transform? This means taking the position that without developing a deeper awareness of our own frames of reference and how they shape practice, there is little likelihood that we can foster change in others.

References

Boyd, R. D., and Meyers, J. G. "Transformative Education." *International Journal of Lifelong Education,* 1988, 7, 261–284.

Brookfield, S. "Racializing the Adult Education." *Harvard Educational Review,* 2003, 73, 497–523.

Brooks, A. "Cultures of Transformation." In A. L. Wilson and E. R. Hayes (eds.), *Handbook of Adult and Continuing Education.* San Francisco: Jossey-Bass, 2000.

Carter, T. J. "The Importance of Talk to Midcareer Women's Development: A Collaborative Inquiry." *Journal of Business Communication,* 2002, 39, 55–91.

Chimera, K. D. "The Use of Reflective Journals in the Promotion of Reflection and Learning in Post-Registration Nursing Students." *Nurse Education Today,* 2006, 27, 192–202.

Christopher, S., Dunnagan, T., Duncan, S. F., and Paul, L. "Education for Self-Support: Evaluating Outcomes Using Transformative Learning Theory." *Family Relations,* 2001, 50, 134–142.

Courtenay, B., Merriam, S. B., and Reeves, P. M. "The Centrality of Meaning-Making in Transformational Learning: How HIV-Positive Adults Make Sense of Their Lives." *Adult Education Quarterly*, 1998, *48*, 65–84.

Cragg, C. E., Plotnikoff, R. C., Hugo, K., and Casey, A. "Perspective Transformation in RN-to-BSN Distance Education." *Journal of Nursing Education*, 2001, *40*(7), 317–322.

Cranton, P. "Individual Differences and Transformative Learning." In J. Mezirow and Associates (eds.), *Learning as Transformation*. San Francisco: Jossey-Bass, 2000.

Daloz, L. *Effective Teaching and Mentoring: Realizing the Transformational Power of Adult Learning Experiences*. San Francisco: Jossey-Bass, 1986.

Dirkx, J. "Transformative Learning Theory in the Practice of Adult Education: An Overview." *PAACE Journal of Lifelong Learning*, 1998, 7, 1–14.

Dirkx, J. "Transformative Learning and the Journey of Individuation." *ERIC Digests*, 2000, no. 223. (ERIC Document Reproduction Service no. ED448305.)

Dirkx, J. M. (2006). "Engaging Emotions in Adult Learning: A Jungian Perspective on Emotion and Transformative Learning." In E. W. Taylor (ed.), *Teaching for Change*. New Directions for Adult and Continuing Education, no. 109. San Francisco: Jossey-Bass, 2006.

Eisen, M. J. "Peer-Based Professional Development Viewed Through the Lens of Transformative Learning." *Holistic Nursing Practice*, 2001, 16, 30–42.

Freire, P. *Pedagogy of the Oppressed*. New York: Continuum, 1984.

Freire, P., and Macedo, D. P. "A Dialogue: Culture, Language, Race." *Harvard Educational Review*, 1995, 65, 377–402.

Janik, D. S. *Unlock the Genius Within*. Lanham, Md.: Rowman and Littlefield Education, 2005.

Janik, D. S. "What Every Language Teacher Should Know About the Brain and How It Affects Teaching." Paper presented at Wikipedia 2007 Conference on Foreign Language Pedagogy, University of Helsinki, Finland, 2007.

Johnson-Bailey, J., and Alfred, M. "Transformational Teaching and the Practices of Black Women Adult Educators." In E. W. Taylor (ed.), *Fostering Transformative Learning in the Classroom: Challenges and Innovations*. New Directions in Adult and Continuing Education, no 109. San Francisco: Jossey-Bass, 2006.

Kegan, R. *In over Our Heads*. Cambridge, Mass.: Harvard University Press, 1994.

Kreber, C. "An Analysis of Two Models of Reflection and Their Implications for Educational Development." *International Journal for Academic Development*, 2004, 9, 29–49.

Lange, E. "Transformative and Restorative Learning: A Vital Dialectic for Sustainable Societies." *Adult Education Quarterly*, 2004, 54, 121–139.

MacLeod, R. D., Parkin, C., Pullon, S., and Robertson, G. "Early Clinical Exposure to People Who Are Dying: Learning to Care at the End of Life." *Medical Education*, 2003, 37, 51–58.

Merriam, S. B. (ed.). *The New Update of Adult Learning Theory*. New Directions of Adult and Continuing Education, no. 89. San Francisco: Jossey-Bass, 2001.

Merriam, S. B. "The Role of Cognitive Development in Mezirow's Transformational Learning Theory." *Adult Education Quarterly*, 2004, 55, 60–68.

Mezirow, J. "Perspective Transformation." *Adult Education*, 1978, *28*, 100–110.

Mezirow, J. *Transformative Dimensions of Adult Learning*. San Francisco: Jossey-Bass, 1991.

Mezirow, J. "Transformation Theory of Adult Learning." In M. R. Welton (ed.), *In Defense of the Lifeworld*. Albany: SUNY Press, 1995.

Mezirow, J. "Contemporary Paradigms of Learning." *Adult Education Quarterly*, 1996, *46*, 158–172.

Mezirow, J. "Transformative Learning: Theory to Practice." In P. Cranton (ed.), *Transformative Learning in Action: Insights from Practice*. New Directions for Adult and Continuing Education, no. 74. San Francisco: Jossey-Bass, 1997.

Mezirow, J., and Associates (eds.). *Learning as Transformation*. San Francisco: Jossey-Bass, 2000.

O'Sullivan, E. *Transformative Learning: Educational Vision for the 21st Century*. London: Zed Books, 1999.

Scribner, J. P., and Donaldson, J. F. "The Dynamics of Group Learning in a Cohort: From Nonlearning to Transformative Learning." *Educational Administration Quarterly*, 2001, 37, 605–638.

Sheared, V. "Giving Voice: An Inclusive Model of Instruction—A Womanist Perspective." In E. Hayes and S.A.J. Colin III (eds.), *Confronting Racism and Sexism in Adult Education*. New Directions for Continuing Education, no. 61. San Francisco: Jossey-Bass, 1994.

Taylor, E. W. (1993). *A Learning Model of Becoming Interculturally Competent: A Transformative Process*. Unpublished dissertation, University of Georgia.

Taylor, E. W. "Transformative Learning: A Critical Review." *ERIC Clearinghouse on Adult, Career, and Vocational Education* (Information Series no. 374), 1998.

Taylor, E. W. "Attending Graduate School in Adult Education and the Impact on Teaching Beliefs: A Longitudinal Study." *Journal of Transformative Education*, 2003, 1(4), 349–368.

Taylor, E. W. (ed). "The Challenge of Teaching for Change." In E. W. Taylor (eds.), *Teaching for Change: Fostering Transformative Learning in the Classroom*. New Directions in Adult and Continuing Education, no. 109. San Francisco: Jossey-Bass, 2006.

Taylor, E. W. "An Update of Transformative Learning Theory: A Critical Review of the Empirical Research (1999–2005)." *International Journal of Lifelong Education*, 2007, 26(2), 173–191.

Tennant, M. C. "The Psychology of Adult Teaching and Learning." In J. M. Peters and P. Jarvis and Associate (eds.), *Adult Education: Evolution and Achievements in a Developing Field of Study*. San Francisco: Jossey-Bass, 1991.

Tisdell, E. J. *Exploring Spirituality and Culture in Adult and Higher Education*. San Francisco: Jossey-Bass, 2003.

Tisdell, E. J. "Feminism." In L. M. English (ed.), *International Encyclopedia of Adult Education*. London: Palgrave, 2005.

Williams, S. H. "Black Mama Sauce: Integrating the Theatre of the Oppressed and Afrocentricity in Transformative Learning." In C. A. Wiessner, S. R. Meyer, N. L. Pfhal, and P. G. Neaman (eds.), *Proceedings of the Fifth International Conference on Transformative Learning*, 2003.

Ziegahn, L. "'Talk' About Culture Online: The Potential for Transformation." *Distance Education*, 2001, 22, 114–150.

Ziegler, M. F., Paulus, T. M., and Woodside, M. "This Course Is Helpful Us All Arrive at New Viewpoints, Isn't It?" *Journal of Transformative Education*, 2006, 4, 302–319.

EDWARD W. TAYLOR *is an associate professor in the adult education doctoral program of the School of Behavioral Sciences and Education at Penn State University-Harrisburg.*

2

This chapter outlines recent research in four areas that can help us rethink workplace learning: definitions, practice-based system perspectives, identities and literacies, and power and politics in workplace learning.

Workplace Learning: Emerging Trends and New Perspectives

Tara Fenwick

The most pressing issues of workplace learning for adult educators have tended to fall into two main categories. The first is figuring out how people solve workplace problems through learning, problems that have become increasingly complex and difficult even to recognize, through learning. These problems can range from integrating new technologies and improving flow of work processes to getting interdisciplinary teams to work together, stopping inequities and prejudices in the workplace, or making people aware of their own power to change the conditions of their work. Educators, being people of action rather than simply social scientists gazing in fascination at the world, tend to use what they find out about people learning in work to help other people learn. So knowledge about workplace learning processes often turns quickly into knowledge about workplace pedagogy.

The second category of issues in workplace learning that tend to pre-occupy adult educators has to do with understanding how particular groups of workers learn. The groups that have attracted most educators' attention tend to be marginalized populations, mainly because there is concern about the access of these populations to meaningful, humane work and decent incomes. Therefore, lots of attention recently has focused on the learning processes and learning needs of groups such as older workers, persons with disabilities, racialized groups, new immigrant workers, low-income workers in precarious work, and so on.

Both of these issue categories have influenced a shift in conceptions of workplace learning toward those discussed in this article: practice-based

NEW DIRECTIONS FOR ADULT AND CONTINUING EDUCATION, no. 119, Fall 2008 © 2008 Wiley Periodicals, Inc.
Published online in Wiley InterScience (www.interscience.wiley.com) • DOI: 10.1002/ace.302

systemic perspectives, identity and literacy theories, and concepts of power and politics.

Beyond adult educators, other groups have focused strong interest on understanding workplace learning processes as well as workplace pedagogies—ways to better teach, support, plan, organize, coach, and enhance workplace learning. Human resource development professionals, for example, have a distinct body of literature exploring workplace learning processes that is aimed at developing organizations, individuals, and careers, and generally improving productivity and well being. Business and management professionals have also become keenly interested in workplace learning in recent decades, examining processes through which groups develop, share and store knowledge, improve practices, and solve problems. In fact, the nature and organization of work has changed so rapidly in the past decade with the effects of globalization that *learning* has become a lightning rod, attracting all sorts of new attention outside educational debates. All the emphasis on the so-called knowledge economy has created demand for innovation—people learning to be creative and entrepreneurial—as a way to stay competitive. New technologies and environments have fundamentally changed what and how people learn in work. Organizations all over North America and Europe are pressed to integrate migrant workers, invoking important issues of inclusion, equity, gender, and race politics in the workplace that have shaken traditional training orientations in the workplace learning agenda. Therefore it is not surprising that interest in workplace learning has accelerated since the mid-1990s. This has expanded into an assortment of fields including, besides those already mentioned, sociology of work, social technology studies, economics, feminist studies, and industrial relations. Naturally there are overlaps in the concepts of workplace learning afoot among these groups, although each tends to frame these learning concepts according to its own distinct purposes.

In this article, the discussion focuses on *learning processes* in the workplace from concepts emerging in the field of adult education, without straying into pedagogies and programs that can enhance learning. Four topics on learning processes seem to be particularly important for addressing key purposes and issues of workplace learning from an adult educator's view: emerging definitions, emerging focus on practice-based learning processes, emerging importance of identity and literacy, and power and politics in learning.

Emerging Definitions and Changing Perspectives

The expansion of workplace issues not only generates new perspectives on learning but also blurs categories. *Learning* can refer to skill acquisition, personal transformation, collective empowerment, or a host of other phenomena. *Workplace* can be an organization, a Website, a kitchen table, even a car. Work varies widely across public, private, and not-for-profit sectors, and among activities of tradesworkers, managers, self-employed profes-sionals, farmers, and domestic workers. Indeed, *work* itself is a slippery cat-egory; it can be paid or unpaid, based in action or reflection, material or virtual, in or out of the home, or more often in various overlapping spaces among these categories. Just as neither workplace nor work can be referred to as some generic, identifiable phenomenon, so does learning in work take multiple forms, faces, and qualities.

In some definitions, the term *workplace learning* has been limited to individual change, with "organizational learning" reserved for groups. How-ever, the problem with this division is that many recent perspectives of learning in work refuse to separate the individual from the collective in examining learning processes. In this article workplace learning refers to relations and dynamics *among* individual actors and collectives. Further, workplace learning here is understood to involve not just human change but interconnections of humans and their actions with rules, tools and texts, cultural, and material environments. Overall, then, workplace learning in this discussion refers not to formal planned training but to "informal" learn-ing. This learning is often *embodied*, not simply mentalist or even involving conscious cognitive activity. It is also often *embedded* in everyday practices, action, and conversation. Learning here is treated not as the outcome of change but as a *process*. In particular, workplace learning can be defined as expanding human possibilities for flexible and creative action in contexts of work.

Emerging Focus on Practice-Based Systemic Learning

Before about 1985, workplace learning was characterized primarily as acqui-sition (Fenwick, 2008); individuals were believed to acquire and store new concepts and skills and behaviors as if knowledge were a package that didn't change in the transfer from its source to the learner's head. Learning workers were understood to be acquiring intellectual capital, increasing the organi-zation's resources, and returning its investment on training. This perspec-tive appears to have completely declined in much workplace literature since about 2001 (Fenwick, 2008). However, more generally, constructivist notions of workplace learning as sense making have become more frequent since the mid-1980s as reflective practice, self-directed learning, transfor-mative learning, and learning style concepts filtered into training literature. Much of this remained focused on the individual, and particularly on the individual's mentalist activity.

In the early 1990s, the concept of a "learning organization" began to emerge in various forms, all of which tried to conceive the relation between the reflecting individual and the active collective in learning processes. The "communities of practice" model, based on ideas first proposed by Etienne Wenger (1998), among others, has been widely taken up in workplace studies. Learning is viewed as the ongoing refinement of practices and emerging knowledge embodied in the specific action of a particular community. Individuals learn *as* they participate in everyday activity within a community (with its history, assumptions and cultural values, rules, and patterns of relationship), with the tools at hand (including objects, technology, language), and in the moment's activity (its purposes, norms, and practical challenges).

This practice-based systemic orientation was taken up more widely as models of "co-participation" and "co-emergence" were applied to understand learning in work. In these conceptions, individual and social learning processes are viewed as enmeshed. Another example is cultural-historical activity theory (CHAT), long popular in Nordic research of workplace learning but just recently introduced into North American literature (Sawchuk, Duarte, and Elhammoumi, 2006). In this view, the workplace is a system of activity shaped by its "object," which is the central problem space at which action is directed. The object could be providing learning opportunities to students that balance societal needs and their own with limited resources in the case of a university department. Or it could be delivering or producing the maximum possible barrels of oil while respecting community needs for employment and environmental protection in the case of a crude oil sands plant. The everyday action of work and learning is further shaped by the system's division of labor, community relationships, rules, tools, and cultural norms as well as the perspectives of the actors within it. CHAT theorists look carefully at the system's *culture* and its *history*–how things came to be as they are and came to be viewed as they are. They also focus on the *contradictions* that all systems carry within them. For example, many work systems carry simultaneous pressures to innovate and take risks while performing with excellence, mastery, and no error. Other work systems also demand greater and greater production to increase profit even though excess production lowers the value of products and increases the value of labor, both of which reduce profit. Here we can see how CHAT retains its Marxist influences in this recognition of the inherent contradictions in capitalist work systems based on labor exchange and the historical emergence of particular practices (Chaiklin, Hedegaard, and Jensen, 2003).

From a CHAT perspective, learning is viewed as expansion of the system's object and reconfiguration of the system's practices. Further, learning combines collective expansion and innovation with individual expansion in conceptions, interactions, and practices. The expansion often comes about through the successive exacerbation and resolution of contradictions within the system. For example, within an organization that promotes collaborative work but gives most rewards to individual effort, some people might begin to seriously question the contradictions at play and their consequences. In a research-intensive university department, these questions could ultimately become directed at the overall object driving their research. Is the object more to generate refereed journal publications and grants, or more to create networked relationships and to have an impact on practice, if these two directions come into conflict? Is the object measured through visible short-term outcomes in place of ambiguous and unpredictable long-term outcomes, even when the latter may be more salient to deeper-impact research? Such questions, taken up seriously throughout the organization, cause the object to expand and shift as individuals' understandings expand and shift.

A third perspective is complexity theory, which has surfaced in organizational studies as a useful way to understand how activity, knowledge, and communities emerge together in the process of workplace learning. Individual interactions and meanings form part of the workplace context itself; they are interconnected systems nested within the larger systems in which they act. The core concept is emergence: knowledge, phenomena, events, and actors are mutually dependent, mutually constitutive, and actually emerge together (Davis and Sumara, 2001). As workers, for example, are influenced by symbols and actions that touch their everyday work, they adapt and learn. As they do so, their behaviors, their meanings, and thus their effects on the systems connected with them change. The focus is not on the components of experience (which other perspectives might describe in fragmented terms: person, experience, tools, and activity) but on the *relationships* binding them together. Workplace learning is the continuous and dynamic invention within these relationships that enable a complex system to flourish in changing environments. For example, studies reported in *Reading Work* (Belfiore and others, 2004) found floor workers' continuous experimentation in diverse workplaces. Hotel cleaning staff invented their own accountability system of codes and recording that was efficient, flexible, and politically astute. Textile workers responded to new ISO-9000 requirements through various inventions of uptake and subterfuge to meet the contradictory demands of increased weaving production while stopping to complete written reports. Such examples show that learning can also be occasioned by disturbances from within or outside the system that become amplified, causing emergence of new, expanded, and more resilient patterns. Further, nothing is predictable; in emergence, the whole is greater than the sum of its parts and is therefore not predictable from examining the parts or the relationships.

Thinking critically, one finds that some of these practice-based orientations to workplace learning bypass questions of politics and power relations: Who is excluded from the construction of knowledge in a community of practice? What dysfunctional or exploitive practices are perpetuated in communities of practice? What hierarchical relations in the workplace reproduce processes of privilege and prejudice? At issue is the extent to which practice-based or social learning theories-including notions of communities of practice, complex adaptive systems, or even CHAT-suppress or enable core questions about the politics and purposes of workplace learning.

New Directions for Adult and Continuing Education • DOI: 10.1002/ace

Emerging Importance of Identities and Literacies

Work communities are powerful sites of identity, where individual workers' desires for recognition, competence, participation, and meaning are both generated and satisfied. Identity is ultimately a representation or mental conception that we ascribe to ourselves and to others: "Our conception of who we are, our identity, is constituted by the power of all of the discursive practices in which we speak—which in turn 'speak' us" (Chappell and others, 2003, p. 41).

People's sense of their own knowledge in work and the knowledge valued by the group to which they see themselves belonging form a critical element of their sense of identity. Identity work itself involves learning. Workers figure out how to position themselves in an organization, how to perform identities that are acceptable to their immediate peers but also allow them freedom and some autonomy and control. In work environments of rapid change where people must transform their practices, people often learn to "shapeshift": they literally learn to perform different selves and knowledges in different environments, while learning to establish some coherent identity to anchor themselves, or even market themselves.

Researchers have explored how particular identities are created among these forces, and how learning processes are involved (Billett, Fenwick, and Somerville, 2007). One case studied miners compelled to transform their work from manual labor in heavy equipment operation to computerized manipulation of equipment using joysticks in an office. At issue were the men's macho-masculine identities, which were no longer relevant. Overall, adult education researchers are interested in how people come to recognize the limitations of their current work identities, how they recognize possibilities for new identities, and what strategies they learn to cope with repressive constraints on their work identities.

Language and literacy are closely related to identity and learning. People's sense of whom they are and what they know and can do at work is embedded in the language and textual practices they use. One area of workplace research examines how learning is shaped by particular written texts in changing workplace environments such as documents, policies, record-keeping forms, and employee growth plans. Such texts standardize what counts as knowledge, thus controlling the work practices and working relations of the people employed (Farrell and Fenwick, 2007). Common examples are the form filling required by new global standardization systems and the accent training given in call centers to make all non-American workers sound American on the telephone. New literacy practices have also been created in the shift to self-directed team arrangements. Workers used to hierarchical communication pipelines have had to learn how to participate productively in team meetings—how to set goals, analyze, and assess collective work through leaderless reflective team dialogues. As people are pressed

New Directions for Adult and Continuing Education • DOI: 10.1002/ace

to learn these new literacies in their work, their sense of self shifts along with how they conceptualize and do their work.

Power and Politics in Workplace Learning

Calls for research to uncover power relations in workplace learning have not resulted in much empirical research. In the literature review of nine journals from 1999 to 2005 (Fenwick, 2008) only about 15 percent of published articles touched on power or politics, and most of them presented theory rather than empirical study. Five perspectives of power appear to be represented among them. In the *radical view*, organizations are viewed as sites of central contradictions and ideological struggle between those who control the means of production and those whose labor and knowledge are exploited. In the *discursive view*, power is viewed as circulating through regimes of knowledge and discursive practices. Power is not possessed by particular people or institutions but is constantly created and readjusted through relations among people and practices, notions of what is normal and what is valuable. Workers participate in and help to sustain the very regimes that discipline and repress their identities and opportunities.

In the *identity politics view*, power relations consolidate a dominant workplace culture whose practices and beliefs actively marginalize or even persecute individuals by virtue of their gender, race, religion, sexual orientation, or conformance to the ability norm valued by the dominant. The *micropolitics view* analyzes power relations as confined to individual strategies to improve their own advantage, such as gamesmanship. Finally, the *community view* avoids critical analysis of structures, knowledge politics, or even interpersonal politics; power is viewed as benign energy, exercised mainly in mobilizing individuals around shared vision, mutual engagement, and sense of belonging.

Adult education analyses of work tend mostly to feature the radical and identity politics views of power, so further discussion of these two is warranted to show their links to learning. In the radical view, workplace learning is often envisioned as radical transformation among workers— empowerment purposed toward workplace reform. Radical or "emancipatory" learning involves workers first in critically analyzing existing repressive conditions of work, including mechanisms in place for controlling knowledge and the means of production (Bratton and others, 2003). Then strategies for resistance and change are generated collectively, in a learning process that builds solidarity, individual and collective agency, and workers' capacity to defend their rights. This learning process of transformation is often positioned in opposition to reproduction, where workers learn to accept and even support exploitive, hierarchical structures that subjugate them and reproduce existing (inequitable) power relations. However, some have argued that this traditional dualism may be overly simplistic, that research needs to examine how reproductive and transformative learning are entwined in everyday work and with what workers themselves want to learn.

In critical workplace learning research adopting an identity politics view of power, issues of race, disability, sexual orientation, and religion are almost completely absent despite their growing importance in other areas of adult education. Gender, on the other hand, has received substantial attention. Studies show that women continue to confront gendered training structures in organizations that are based on patriarchal values, male-oriented communication patterns, and family-unfriendly schedules. Women in particular are often expected to nurture the close relationships and community that organizations want, mentor others, and display cheerfulness (Mojab and Gorman, 2003). Yet the learning valued and supported most in organizations tends to be related more to leadership and innovation in professional and managerial jobs, where women continue to be underrepresented. Meanwhile, women who are new immigrants and of color are overrepresented in precarious, contingent employment such as call center, food service, and home-based work, where there are few learning opportunities to help women obtain better-paying and more secure employment.

Finally, an important emerging line of research incorporates considerations of space and spatiality into analyses of power and learning in workplaces, borrowing from critical geography (Hearn and Michelson, 2006). Space is not considered a static container into which work and workers are poured, but a dynamic multiplicity that is constantly being produced by simultaneous "stories-so-far." One simple example from my own experience: private offices were constructed for government social service officers at their own request, for reasons of noise, privacy, and overall stress reduction. This severely reduced casual information flow and relational connections among these officers. The need was met through formal meetings and increased reliance on written memos and e-mail, which served to increase workload and stress and reduce ongoing informal experimentation. Issues for learning and work include how spaces are constituted in ways that enable or inhibit learning, create inequities or exclusions, and open or limit possibilities for new practices and knowledge. Particularly in new work arrangements such as virtual organizations and transnational work sites, space and time have become a critical influence on work learning. We need to ask, What knowledge counts where, and how does it emerge in different time-spaces? How are identities negotiated through movements and locations? How is learning enmeshed in the making of spaces?

Future Directions

Workplace learning is contested terrain filled with fundamental tensions related to what knowledge counts most and who says so. When we read various theories and studies of workplace learning, we can see how perspectives are shifting about what constitutes knowledge, how workers are connected to one another and to their environments, and how action and reflection are related. More important, researchers and educators promote differing purposes for workplace learning that influence how learning is understood. Some focus on individual human development, some on building solidarity and political consciousness among workers, and others are more interested in "upskilling" workers and productivity. Other differences in perspective arise from the unit of analysis. Those who focus on the individual might explain learning as developing expertise or transforming beliefs. Those who focus on the system might examine social learning processes and change occurring in practices among the group. These different perspectives are not necessarily irreconcilable, but neither do they nest neatly into one another. No single model for workplace learning is acceptable in the face of such distinct positions.

The three emerging areas described in this chapter have become particularly important in guiding future research: practice-based systemic views, identities and literacy, and power and politics in work-related learning. Of all the ideas currently afloat in adult education addressing work issues, these trends seem most likely to influence future perspectives, program design, and pedagogical practice in workplace learning. Overall, we have a great need for rigorous in-depth empirical research that traces what people actually do and think in everyday work activity, and for research methods that can help illuminate the learning that unfolds in everyday work. Such research could help us counter the plethora of books that present a depoliticized, morally infused prescription for what we ought to do to "promote learning" in current workplaces, and it may even help expand possibilities for what work and spaces of work could become in our future.

References

Belfiore, M. E., and others. *Reading Work: Literacies in the New Workplace*. Mahwah, N.J.: Erlbaum, 2004.

Billett, S., Fenwick, T., and Somerville, M. (eds.). *Work, Learning and Subjectivity*. New York: Springer, 2007.

Bratton, J., Mills, J. H., Pyrch, T., and Sawchuk, P. *Workplace Learning: A Critical Introduction*. Aurora, Ont.: Garamond Press, 2003.

Chaiklin, S., Hedegaard, M., and Jensen, U. J. *Activity Theory and Social Practice: Cultural Historical Approaches*. Langelandsgade, Denmark: Aarhus Press, 2003.

Chappell, C., and others. *Reconstructing the Lifelong Learner: Pedagogy and Identity in Individual, Organisational and Social Change*. London: Routledge Falmer, 2003.

Davis, B., and Sumara, D. "Learning Communities: Understanding the Workplace as a Complex System." In T. Fenwick (ed.), *Socio-Cultural Understandings of Workplace Learning*. New Directions in Adult and Continuing Education, no. 92. San Francisco: Jossey-Bass, 2001.

Farrell, L., and Fenwick, T. "Educating the Global Workforce?" In L. Farrell and T. Fenwick (eds.), *Educating the Global Workforce*. London: Routledge, 2007.

Fenwick, T. "Understanding Relations of Individual-Collective Learning in Work: A Review of Research." *Management Learning*, 2008, 39(3), 227–243.

Hearn, M., and Michelson, G. *Rethinking Work: Time, Space and Discourse.* Cambridge, UK: Cambridge University Press, 2006.

Sawchuk, P., Duarte, N., and Elhammoumi, M. *Critical Perspectives on Activity: Explorations Across Education, Work, and Everyday Life.* New York: Cambridge University Press, 2006.

Wenger, E. *Communities of Practice: Learning, Meaning and Identity.* Cambridge, UK: Cambridge University Press, 1998.

TARA FENWICK is professor and head of the Department of Educational Studies at the University of British Columbia.

3

The role of spirituality in adult education and adult learning is discussed by defining spirituality *and exploring how spiritual experience facilitates spiritual development.*

Spirituality and Adult Learning

Elizabeth J. Tisdell

"What do you mean by spirituality?" This is a question I've often heard in the past decade as I tell people of my research interest in the role of spirituality in learning in adult and higher education. Typically, there are three follow-up responses. The first is often another question: "Is spirituality the same as religion?" The second is a look (often from other academics) that seems to indicate they wonder if I'm some sort of new age flake. The third is something like, "Oh, that's fascinating!" which often results in a continued conversation where the person shares a significant spiritual experience and what was learned from it.

Spirituality is currently a hot topic. There are numerous responses among adult and higher education scholars to its current interest by society at large, some similar to those just noted. Many agree with bell hooks (2000) when she suggests that it's time to "break mainstream cultural taboos that silence our passion for spiritual practice" (p. 82). But there are others who wonder, as Robert Wuthnow (1998) observes, "whether 'spiritual' has become synonymous with 'flaky'" (p. 1). The subject of spirituality is still somewhat marginalized in the academy, but since the new millennium there's been a growing discussion about its role both in higher education (Chickering, Dalton, and Stamm, 2005; Dillard, 2006; hooks, 2000, 2003) and in adult education (English and Gillen, 2000; English, Fenwick and Parsons, 2003; Tisdell, 2003; Tolliver and Tisdell, 2006).

The purpose of this chapter is to consider the important influence that spirituality has in adult learning and how discussions of it are affecting the field of adult education. In so doing, I'll begin by attempting to define spirituality and then consider the nature of spiritual experience and its

NEW DIRECTIONS FOR ADULT AND CONTINUING EDUCATION, no. 119, Fall 2008 © 2008 Wiley Periodicals, Inc.
Published online in Wiley InterScience (www.interscience.wiley.com) • DOI: 10.1002/ace.303

relationship to adult development. Finally, I'll conclude with some brief implications for practice.

Defining Spirituality in Adult Education

Defining *spirituality* is a somewhat elusive task; it means different things to different people, and there is often some confusion between "spirituality" and "religion." Generally, in contemporary literature spirituality is about an *individual's* personal experience with the sacred, which can be experienced anywhere. Religion, on the other hand, is about an *organized community of faith*, with an official creed, and codes of regulatory behavior.

Most contemporary scholars who write about spirituality focus on its role in an *individual's* creation of ultimate meaning, usually in relationship to a higher sense of self or what is referred to as "God," "Divine Spirit," "Lifeforce," or "Great Mystery." Many also highlight its connection to wholeness and the more authentic self. Faith development theorist James Fowler (1981) emphasizes the significance of unconscious processes in how individuals make meaning of ultimate reality. He notes the significance of image, symbol, metaphor, music, or kinesthetic sensory experience that is beyond the cognitive or rational realm as central to those meaning-making processes that people often connect to as the spiritual. A participant in my own study of adult educators' spirituality described it as "a journey toward wholeness"; he then went on to use language full of symbols and metaphor to try to find ways of expressing that wholeness. But if spirituality is about wholeness, and because the whole is always greater than the sum of the parts, then spirituality itself is always greater than that which can be described in language. When defined as a journey or an experience leading toward wholeness, everyone has a spirituality (including agnostics and atheists), but not everyone has a religion.

Spirituality and Religion

The distinction just made between spirituality and religion—that spirituality is about an individual's personal experience or journey toward wholeness, whereas religion is about an organized community of faith—seems clear enough at first blush. But in reality, it's not quite as simple as that, for three primary reasons. First, most of us were socialized in a religious tradition, and the earliest stage of our spiritual development took place within the context of that particular religion. Thus, even if we have long since left the religion in which we grew up, our earliest religious training affects our understanding of our spirituality as a "journey toward wholeness" at a foundational level, because it is the beginning stage of that journey.

Second, although religions are communities of faith with an official creed and rules of regulatory behavior, they do offer guidance on how to live a spiritual life and have personal experiences of the sacred. They also come with rituals, music, symbols, prayers, and sacred stories that connect with or honor many of life's transitions that serve as gateways to the sacred. Thus for many of us some spiritual experiences might have taken place or been ritualized and given further meaning in the context of our religious traditions. In such instances, it might be difficult to separate spiritual experience from one's religion.

A third source of confusion between religion and spirituality has to do with the interchangeable use of the terms in some literature, particularly that which is less contemporary. But if one remembers that spirituality is primarily about an individual's experience whereas religion is about an organized community of faith, it's possible to glean whether an author is really talking about religion or spirituality. Used as nouns, the terms *spirituality* and *religion* differ in the ways I have just noted. But when the adjective *religious* is used to describe an *individual's* experience or imaginative work (as in "religious experience" or "religious imagination"), the meaning of the terms *religious* and *spiritual* is equivalent. In short, spirituality is about experience, and when the term *religious* is used in relation to experience, the author is likely talking about what contemporary writers would call spirituality. Thus, if William James (1902/1982) were writing his famous book *The Varieties of Religious Experience* today as opposed to a century ago, he probably would title it "The Varieties of Spiritual Experience."

Spirituality in Adult Education

Spirituality has historically had quite an important influence in the adult education field (English, 2005), though often the connection has been more implicit. Even though spirituality is generally seen as an individual's experiences of what is perceived as sacred, how one frames or understands those experiences can strongly influence one's beliefs and behaviors. In living out their spirituality, some people focus more on its inward activities such as prayer, meditation, and experiences of wholeness; others focus more on how it influences their outer action in the world, and they might not discuss spirituality per se unless asked about it directly. As Leona English (2005) points out, where the influence of spirituality has been particularly strong historically in the field is in its abiding influence in the lives of well-known social justice educators whose work has shaped the field. Myles Horton of the Highlander Folk School and Paulo Freire of the emancipatory education movement, like many others, were strongly influenced by the Christian social gospel; it was a strong underpinning to their social justice work. The focus of their work as adult educators, however, was on educating for social change, as opposed to directly discussing spirituality. Similarly, it was an abiding influence on Jimmy Tompkins and Moses Coady of the Nova Scotia Antigonish movement.

In more recent years, this implicit influence of spirituality in adult education has become more explicit in that there's more direct discussion of it. This influence has been felt in four primary ways. First, a significant number of adult education professors have had earlier careers in ministry. Jarvis and Walters (1993) edited a book in which the contributors examined how theology and spirituality influenced their educational philosophy and their work overall. Second, more recent writers have discussed the influence of spirituality and soul in how it affects learning on an individual level (Dirkx, 1997, 2001; English and Gillen, 2000; Hunt, 2001). A third influence is in the arena of workplace learning, where authors focus on how it influences how they think and act in the professional workplace or in working for the common good as leaders and educators (Bolman and Deal, 1995; Daloz, Keen, Keen, and Parks, 1994; Conger, 1994; English, Fenwick, and Parsons, 2003; Fox, 1995). However, as Fenwick and Lange (1998) have pointed out, some of the wider literature on spirituality in the workplace has an emphasis on individual needs and organizational development for the purposes of profit rather than a focus on the common good. Finally, the strong influence of spirituality is still present in those educating for social justice in myriad adult education settings (Clover, Follen, and Hall, 1998; Dillard, 2006; English, 2005; Tisdell, 2003; Tolliver and Tisdell, 2006).

Spiritual Experience and Spiritual Development

As William James noted a century ago, there are a variety of spiritual experiences. From an adult education perspective, this connects to the area of experiential learning. Just as in any experience that leads to learning, a spiritual experience takes place at a particular *moment in time*. But making sense of it or learning from the experience happens over time. This is where it connects to spiritual *development*, because development is generally conceptualized as change over time (Merriam, Caffarella, and Baumgartner, 2007). How these moments in time relate to change over time is considered here in light of the nature of spiritual experience.

Learning Through Spiritual Experience

Life is full of ups and downs. Sometimes it's rather ordinary, at other times chaotic. Spirituality helps us see the extraordinary in the ordinary business of life, and spiritual experiences can create a new order out of chaos, or jazz out of discord. Sharon Welch (1999) noted in her discussion of spirituality that the famous jazz pianist Mary Lou Williams would occasionally pause in midperformance to make audiences more attentive: "Listen! This will heal you!" (p. 19) she would say. This admonition, no doubt, got people's attention and helped them listen in a new way. Significant spiritual experiences are like that.

New Directions for Adult and Continuing Education • DOI: 10.1002/ace

Some people report having spiritual experiences all the time. But *significant* spiritual experiences of deep learning seem to happen only occasionally. Such experiences offer hope, healing, or affirmation, as if to say, just like Mary Lou Williams's admonition to her audiences, "Listen! This will heal you! This will teach you something new." They stand out as "shimmering moments" in our lives—moments that we often go back to with awe and wonder. The ongoing power of their "shimmer" endures as we continue to make meaning. These are often moments of significant learning that lead to continued development.

There are many types of shimmering moments. In my study of how spirituality informs the lives and practices of thirty-one culturally diverse adult educators (Tisdell, 2003), the participants discussed several types of significant spiritual learning experiences. The first set of spiritual experiences reported seems to speak to the universality of human experience across culture. Giving birth or witnessing one, being present at a death, or having a close brush with one's own potential death, resulting in a new sense of life purpose, are examples. A second set were reports of significant nighttime dreams and daytime synchronicities (those odd coincidences Jung talked about that seem more than coincidental). These sacred moments offered new learning about hope, healing, or direction in times of difficulty; brought elation and joy in times of celebration; facilitated or affirmed a life decision; or spoke to the interconnectedness of everything.

A third type were those that took place in nature or in meditation. These created a sense of learning about the value of centering and affirmed a sense of wholeness and the interconnectedness of everything. Some spoke of these as experiences of bliss. Those who were engaged in a regular spiritual practice, as through regular prayer or mindfulness meditation genres, suggested that their practice helped them learn to cultivate attention to the spiritual, to see the extraordinary in the ordinary business of life. They reported that they often had spiritual experiences in meditation, but the most *significant* spiritual experiences happened in the context of living their lives.

A final type of spiritual experience was related to the ongoing development of some aspect of identity. These were reported much more often by women and people of color. For example, many of the women discussed developing a more positive gender identity over time through deconstructing the patriarchy of some of their childhood religious traditions, and then reclaiming aspects of those traditions through a more woman-positive spirituality lens. Similarly, people of color discussed learning some of the history and spirituality of their own cultures of origin, resulting in reclaiming a more positive cultural identity overall.

The spiritual part of those experiences was when they reclaimed aspects of the sacred in their own cultural or gender story, or found new power in reframing some of the cultural symbols, mythic stories, music, or metaphors that were part of their earlier life experience. In this sense, they spiraled back to reframe earlier experiences that not only yielded a greater sense of creativity but also facilitated healing from oppression of themselves and others from their cultural communities. Many discussed these experiences as helping them learn to be their more authentic self in light of their more integrated sense of identity.

Mary Catherine Bateson (1995) calls spiraling-back experiences of this kind, where people reflect back on old experiences and discover something new, "spiral learning." What may have been peripheral to these earlier learning experiences can become an important meaning-making opportunity at a later date, through the process of spiral learning, whether spiritual or not. But just as events and experiences of the past can be infused and remapped with new meaning, so too can symbols, mythic story, metaphor, and music. For the participants in my study, when these spiral-learning experiences were infused with the stuff of symbol, mythic story, metaphor, or music, they were often discussed as spiritual experiences and were seen as transformative as well as spiritual.

Spiritual Experience Fostering Spiritual Development

Much of the learning from these types of spiritual experiences, especially from spiral learning, resulted in further spiritual development, as well as development of the overall self. This is likely because such experiences facilitated a more integrated sense of identity. Most developmental theorists who write about spiritual development connect it with other aspects of development. James Fowler (1981), known for his linear stage theory of faith development, ties spiritual and faith development strongly to cognitive and moral development, drawing heavily on the work of Piaget and Kohlberg. But he takes issue with them because of their ignoring of "the role of imagination in knowing, their neglect of symbolic processes generally and the related lack of attention to unconscious structuring processes other than those constituting reasoning" (p. 103).

Though Fowler's work has the limitations of all linear stage theories as well as the fact that his sample of 359 was almost entirely made up of white people of the Judeo-Christian tradition, his work highlights the important way in which people construct knowledge through image and symbol, an area that has been ignored by most development and learning theorists. Other writers have drawn on Fowler's work in studying spiritual development at particular life stages. James Loder (1998) discussed it from a theological perspective in relation to various stages of adulthood, whereas Sharon Daloz Parks (2000) deals primarily with young adulthood but also discusses the significance of imagination and the role of constructing knowledge by engaging imagination. Robert Wuthnow (1998, 1999, 2001) has conducted a number of studies about people's conceptions and experiences of spirituality as adults and how it influences their further development. His interesting study (2001) of how artists conceptualize spirituality and how it influences their work and further creativity also gets at the power of symbol and imagination in relation to spirituality.

Whether or not spiritual development unfolds in a series of linear stages is a matter of some debate and, as Wilber (2000) observes, depends on how one defines spirituality. However, he suggests that spiritual development unfolds in overlapping and interweaving levels, "resulting in a meshwork or dynamic spiral of consciousness unfolding" (p. 7). Each level includes and expands on the development of earlier stages and moves to greater integration, which reflects an important theme of spiritual development: the ongoing development of identity. Significant spiritual experiences as specific moments in time, as they are integrated into one's overall life, clearly can lead to further development of identity. This often happens in concert with further cognitive and moral development, through further education or life experience, and is often a process of moving forward and spiraling back to reframe earlier experiences. When participants in my own study described such movement as spiritual, they tended to slip into metaphorical or symbolic language. Perhaps it's the connection to the symbolic and imaginal realms that happens in an experience at a moment in time, helping people tune in to other levels of consciousness that Wilber refers to, and that make people feel something is "spiritual" development as opposed to simply psychological development.

Bateson (1995), in her consideration of spiral learning, and Kegan (1994), in his discussion of the unfolding of the "orders of consciousness," both discuss the spiral shape of development overall. But neither really focuses on the role of spirituality in the process. This idea that spiritual development has a spiral shape not only fits what I saw in my own study but is also present in other authors' and researchers' narratives that get at aspects of spiritual development (Borysenko, 1999; Daloz, Keen, Keen, and Parks, 1996; Loder, 1998; Terkel, 2001; Wade-Gayles, 1995; Wuthnow, 1999, 2001). On the basis of these studies and narratives, adults who value spirituality often describe their adult spiritual development as a process of questioning or moving away from earlier beliefs or experiences from one's childhood religious or cultural tradition, as other ways of being in the world are explored through education or other life experiences related to cognitive and moral development. Then later they spiral back and reframe aspects of those earlier experiences, often in light of mythic or cultural story or other forms of knowledge that tap into creativity.

By the time many who see their lives as a spiritual journey or a journey toward wholeness have reached midlife, they have questioned, doubted, explored other spiritual possibilities, and gone on the journey of reclaiming and spiraling back. They often have embraced the tension of opposites, rather than resorting to either-or thinking that might be characteristic of earlier adulthood; and have more of an ability to live the tensions of the paradox. Tensions often pull us open to new spiritual experience and ways of seeing the world (Palmer, 1980). This often results in a firmer commitment to want to live according to what one sees as one's life's purpose. Although actually living out this commitment is difficult, in many research studies and narratives (Daloz, Keen, Keen, and Parks, 1996; Tisdell, 2003; Wuthnow, 1999, 2001) participants describe doing so as a way of life that required inner reflection, which also led to outer action and a sense of communal responsibility. It's the spiritual experiences as moments in time happening along the way that help people experience life as a journey toward wholeness, that often give people further hope and courage facilitating an ability to live out their commitment, also leading to further spiritual development.

Conclusions and Implications for Adult Education Practice

So what does this mean for adult education practice, where there is often confusion between spirituality and religion? Additionally, many of us are educating in secular places that emphasize "separation of church and state"; what of this? First, attending to spirituality in learning doesn't mean that one need necessarily discuss it directly in classes or learning activities. One can ask learners about the experience of a shimmering moment in their lives, relative to a particular topic, and then explore what was so significant about the experience. This of course doesn't necessarily mean that spirituality will come up. But it creates a space where it may. Of course, what one person calls spiritual, another might call an experience of creativity, and another might call an experience of deep connection.

Second, it's important to keep in mind that people construct knowledge in powerful ways through spiritual experience that leads to further development. There is power in trying to engage people in spiral learning opportunities that draw on multiple realms of being, including the rational; the affective; and the symbolic, imaginal, and spiritual domains. Engaging the latter domains may be important for all learners in some contexts, but it might be particularly important for learners whose cultures have been marginalized; doing so often stimulates creativity for making change and thus gives hope. Walters and Manicom (1996) highlight this point in relation to popular education and emancipatory practices, noting how "culturally distinct groups, women recovering 'womanist' traditions and ethnic collectives, draw on cultural and spiritual symbols in healing and transformative education" (p. 13). The ability to create, imagine, and come to further insight through symbol, metaphor, and art is part of the experience of being human that is so often ignored in education. Thus, making use of these ways of knowing in the educational process might permit many learners to connect to the spiritual realm or their own creativity, as they envision new ways of working for change.

New Directions for Adult and Continuing Education • DOI: 10.1002/ace

Finally, there also may be times when it is perfectly appropriate to directly include spirituality as part of the course content, if it's relevant to one's educational purpose. Our purpose as adult educators is to facilitate learning and nurture development, "to recognize what is already inherent within our relationships and experiences, to acknowledge its presence with the teaching and learning environment, to respect its sacred message" (Dirkx, 1997, p. 83). Similarly, in creating learning communities both hooks (2003) and Palmer (1998) discuss the importance of attending to paradox, sacredness, and graced moments in teaching and learning. This means attending to the shimmering moments in our own teaching and learning in our own journey toward wholeness—times when something beckoned and said "Listen! This will heal you!" By doing that listening, and attending to those shimmering moments as teachers of adults and adult learners ourselves, we might encourage our students to do the same. Indeed, that's part of attending to spirituality in adult learning.

References

Bateson, M. C. *Peripheral Visions*. San Francisco: Harper Perennial, 1995.

Bolman, L. G., and Deal, T. E. *Leading with Soul: An Uncommon Journey of Spirit*. San Francisco: Jossey-Bass, 1995.

Borysenko, J. *A Women's Journey to God*. New York: Riverhead Books, 1999.

Chickering, A., Dalton, J., and Stamm, L. *Encouraging Authenticity and Spirituality in Higher Education*. San Francisco: Jossey-Bass, 2005.

Clover, D., Follen, S., and Hall, B. *The Nature of Transformation: Environmental, Adult and Popular Education*. Toronto, Ont.: Transformative Learning Centre, 1998.

Conger, J., and Associates. *Spirit at Work*. San Francisco: Jossey-Bass, 1994.

Daloz, L., Keen, C., Keen, J., and Parks, S. *Common Fire: Lives of Commitment in a Complex World*. Boston: Beacon, 1996.

Dillard, C. B. *On Spiritual Strivings*. Albany: SUNY Press, 2006.

Dirkx, J. "The Power of Feelings: Emotion, Imagination, and the Construction of Meaning in Adult Learning." In S. Merriam (ed.), *The New Update on Adult Learning Theory*. New Directions for Adult and Continuing Education, no. 89. San Francisco: Jossey-Bass, 2001.

Dirkx, J. M. "Nurturing Soul in Adult Learning." In P. Cranton (ed.), *Transformative Learning in Action*. New Directions for Adult and Continuing Education, no. 74. San Francisco: Jossey-Bass, 1997.

English, L. "Historical and Contemporary Explorations of the Social Change and Spiritual Directions of Adult Education." Teachers College Record, 2005, *107*(6), 1169–1192.

English, L., and Gillen, M. (eds.) *Addressing the Spiritual Dimensions of Adult Learning*. New Directions for Adult and Continuing Education, no. 85. San Francisco: Jossey-Bass, 2000.

English, L. M., Fenwick, T., and Parsons, J. *Spirituality in Adult Education and Training*. Malabar, Fla.: Krieger, 2003.

Fenwick, T. J., and Lange, E. "Spirituality in the Workplace: The New Frontier of HRD." *Canadian Journal for the Study of Adult Education*, 1998, *12*(1), 63–87.

Fowler, J. *Stages of Faith*. San Francisco: Harper and Row, 1981.

Fox, M. *The Reinvention of Work*. San Francisco: HarperCollins, 1995.

hooks, b. *All About Love*. New York: Morrow, 2000.

hooks, b. *Teaching Community*. New York: Routledge, 2003.

Hunt, C. "A Way of Well Being: Approaching Spirituality Through Reflective Practice." *Adult Learning*, 2001, *12*(3), 7–9.

James, W. *The Varieties of Religious Experience*. New York: Penguin Books, 1982. (Originally published in 1902.)

Jarvis, P., and Walters, N. (eds.). *Adult Education and Theological Interpretations*. Malabar, Fla.: Krieger, 1993.

Kegan, R. *In over Our Heads: The Mental Demands of Modern Life*. Cambridge, Mass.: Harvard University Press, 1994.

Loder, J. *The Logic of the Spirit: Human Development in Theological Perspective*. San Francisco: Jossey-Bass, 1998.

Merriam, S., Caffarella, R., and Baumgartner, L. *Learning in Adulthood*. San Francisco: Jossey-Bass, 2007.

Palmer, P. *The Promise of Paradox*. Notre Dame, Ind.: Ave Maria Press, 1980.

Palmer, P. J. *The Courage to Teach*. San Francisco: Jossey-Bass, 1998.

Parks, S. D. *Big Questions, Worthy Dreams*. San Francisco: Jossey-Bass, 2000.

Terkel, S. *Will the Circle Be Unbroken?* New York: New Press, 2001.

Tisdell, E. *Exploring Spirituality and Culture in Adult and Higher Education*. San Francisco: Jossey-Bass, 2003.

Tolliver, D., and Tisdell, E. "Engaging Spirituality in the Transformative Higher Education Classroom." In E. Taylor (ed.), *Teaching for Change: Fostering Transformative Learning in the Classroom*. New Directions for Adult and Continuing Education, no. 109. San Francisco: Jossey Bass, 2006.

Wade-Gayles, G. (ed.). *My Soul Is a Witness: African American Women's Spirituality*. Boston: Beacon Press, 1995.

Walters, S., and Manicom, L. (eds.). *Gender in Popular Education*. London: Zed Press, 1996.

Welch, S. *Sweet Dreams in America: Making Ethics and Spirituality Work*. New York: Routledge, 1999.

Wilber, K. A. A *Theory of Everything*. Boston: Shambhala, 2000.

Wuthnow, R. *After Heaven: Spirituality in America Since the 1950s*. Berkeley: University of California Press, 1998.

Wuthnow, R. *Growing up Religious*. Boston: Beacon Press, 1999.

Wuthnow, R. *Creative Spirituality: The Way of the Artist*. Berkeley: University of California Press, 2001.

ELIZABETH J. TISDELL is associate professor and coordinator of the adult education doctoral program at the Pennsylvania State University, Harrisburg.

Learning through the body is discussed in this chapter as a valued, alternative way of knowing that reconnects the mind and body.

Learning Through the Body

Tammy J. Freiler

In the tragic aftermath of the December 2004 tsunami off the coast of Thailand, a group of nomads known as the Moken village sea gypsies were featured in an investigative report for their high rate of survival along with the animal population (Simon, 2005). In seeking to discover why this particular group of people survived when so many others had perished, the report uncovered a felt, perceptive sense of the Mokens' lived body experiences with their environment that enabled them to recognize and interpret the signs of the sea and responses of living things to environmental nuances as precursors of the impending tsunami.

As a counselor, health educator, and person in the Western world, I was fascinated by how the Mokens knew about the tsunami. Their way of knowing, embedded in their cultural context of interrelatedness with their environment, surfaced as the reason for their survival. Basically they survived the tsunami because they detected the warnings and reacted accordingly. When asked why they thought they survived, a villager explained that it was because they had paid attention to and felt the signs when others did not take the time to notice, or did not know how to notice (Simon, 2005).

Being perceptively attuned to their environment, the Mokens inhabit and experience their world in a way of knowing rooted in their survival that could indicate they make use of what is sometimes referred to as embodied knowing, or embodiment. Bermudez, Marcel, and Eilan (1998) suggest that this type of experiencing could be conceptualized as phenomenological, rooted in the nature and essence of the Mokens' experiencing selves as their way of life resonates with their surroundings.

NEW DIRECTIONS FOR ADULT AND CONTINUING EDUCATION, no. 119, Fall 2008 © 2008 Wiley Periodicals, Inc.
Published online in Wiley InterScience (www.interscience.wiley.com) • DOI: 10.1002/ace.304

I recognize similarities in my own lived body experiences with those of the Mokens. I navigate through each day with a heightened sense of embodied awareness, in a far less dramatic and traumatic sense of survival in line with facilitating wellness in both my personal life and professional role as a counselor and educator. However, I also recognize that, for many individuals, embodiment may mean nothing more than experiencing a sense of bodily, physical presence that is quite detached from knowing. Developing a deeper understanding of exactly what is meant by embodiment and how some of our learning in the world is accessed through embodied experiences can be daunting and perplexing. After all, approaching the body is steeped in complexity.

Although turning to the Mokens' experiences offers initial insights on embodiment, this chapter contributes to a broader understanding of embodiment as a way of knowing, first by explaining how embodiment is conceptualized in the literature, then by describing how experiences of embodiment can be incorporated in learning, and finally by explaining the implications of embodiment and learning related to theory and practice.

The Nature of Embodiment and Learning

Emerging in complex discussions of embodiment is trying to determine exactly what it is as a way of knowing. Is it intuition? The sea gypsies described a felt sense. Is it being perceptively mindful of surroundings? The sea gypsies described their sensory experiences. Or is it perhaps something more encompassing, relational, and holistic that captures the essence of interrelatedness and connection through being-in-the-world as experienced by the Mokens?

Price and Shildrick (1999) discuss embodiment as an interrelated essence, stating, "Instead of the body being positioned as a bar to knowledge, knowledge is produced through the body and embodied ways of being in the world" (p. 19). This description suggests that the Mokens' way of knowing points to their direct experiencing as embodiment. Within direct experience, the physiological and emotional reactions of the stress response, its genetic basis, and maintenance of homeostasis between mind and body point to an innate ability to tap into deep recesses of embodied knowing to effect survival (Damasio, 1999). Striving for survival through the stress response could be considered as one of the most significant universal manifestations of embodiment. However, the report of the sea gypsies made me wonder if most humans, in general, have become inattentive to the potentiality of learning through the body. Has our way of living in modern civilization for the most part tuned us out and turned us off from this way of knowing?

The sea gypsies fluidly described their embodied experiences, but for most people in the Western world how to describe and interpret actually being embodied and experiencing embodiment in the moment remains awkward and challenging. Indeed, we live in a culture that bombards us with unrealistic body images and societal preoccupation with physical appearance and body consciousness. This certainly could account for why many of us have become disconnected from and inattentive to our bodies. Further, until we are faced with a health issue, from aging or illness for example, there is a tendency not to give it much attention. But literature on embodiment is contributing further attention to this phenomenon and permitting emerging insights.

Conceptualizing Embodied Learning. There are varied directions in discourses about embodied learning seeking to explain and understand it as a way of knowing (Merriam, Caffarella, and Baumgartner, 2007). This section discusses several of these directions.

First, *embodiment, embodied learning,* and *somatic learning* are all closely aligned and used interchangeably in the discourses. They are associated with an evolving awareness of bodily experiences as a source of constructing knowledge through engaged, lived body experiences of physicality, sensing, and being in both body and world (Beaudoin, 1999; Brockman, 2001; Clark, 2001). However, as a distinction, somatic learning generally refers to learning directly experienced through bodily awareness and sensation during purposive body-centered movements (Alexander Technique, tai chi, yoga).

Tai chi, for example, is an ancient Eastern practice centered on self-healing and renewal through connections among the body, mind, thought, and inner energy (Lee, Lee, Lee, and Lee, 1996). As an effective practice particularly for stress management, tai chi is a series of slow, self-controlled bodily movements that integrate gentle stretching, diaphragmatic breathing, balance, martial art, dance, meditation, and relaxation. Given that the particular body-centered movements of tai chi have a specific purpose, this type of practice is more often referred to as a form of somatic learning in the literature.

In comparison, embodiment and embodied learning generally refer to a broader, more holistic view of constructing knowledge that engages the body as a site of learning, usually in connection with other domains of knowing (for example, spiritual, affective, symbolic, cultural, rational). Direct engagement in an experience of guided imagery and visualization that connects mental images, bodily sensations, and reactions can be interrelated with other domains of knowing (Freiler, 2007). The nature of experiencing and the learning drawn from the experience are more deeply related to subjective meaning and interpretation than to a purposive intent. Thus, this type of experience is more often referred to as an experience of embodiment or embodied learning.

Second, in noting complex variations of embodiment, Csordas (1994) adds, "most authors regard it as an existential condition, others as a process in which meaning is taken into or upon the body, yet others prefer the term bodiliness over embodiment" (p. 20). Csordas focuses on the experience of being a body and the phenomenon of bodiliness as a way to discuss embodiment. Furthermore, Weiss and Haber (1999) note that "the very expression 'the body' has become problematized," (p. xiv) making embodiment even more complex to understand. From their view, the concept of embodiment is directly associated with "a shift from viewing the body as a nongendered, prediscursive phenomenon that plays a central role in perception, cognition, action, and nature to a way of living or inhabiting the world through one's acculturated body" (p. xiv).

A third direction from cognitive science delineates forms of embodiment through bodily activities and experience (Lakoff and Johnson, 1999). More specifically, phenomenological embodiment is manifest via image schemas with our bodies through bodily projections, orientation, and inhabiting space (spatial relations with objects such as front and back, use and movement of the body to push, pull, and balance). How a person is able to orient or schematize body movements to back a manual transmission car out of a garage or to stumble through a home to grab a flashlight when the lights go out in a power outage could be considered as manifestations of phenomenological embodiment.

Another form of embodiment, referred to as neural embodiment, is tied to neural mechanisms that categorize structures such as color concepts. Both phenomenological and neural embodiment are grounded in concepts of cognitive science, whereby reason is connected to our bodies, brain structures, and environmental interactions and experiences to give us "our sense of what is real" (Lakoff and Johnson, 1999, p. 17). Furthermore, the mind is considered to be embodied in ways that draw meaning "grounded in and through our bodies" (p. 6).

In a fourth direction, embodiment is conceptualized as a way to construct knowledge by incorporating unity of mind and body in the process of knowing through both objective and subjective realms of knowledge construction. The objective realm refers to an externally driven way of processing information through rational structures of reason to construct knowledge, while the subjective realm refers to internally oriented, personal ways of processing information to construct knowledge through thoughts, ideas, and feelings (Simon, 1998).

In summary, for the purpose of this chapter embodiment is defined as a way to construct knowledge through direct engagement in bodily experiences and inhabiting one's body through a felt sense of being-in-the-world. It also involves a sense of connectedness and interdependence through the essence of lived experiencing within one's complete humanness, both body and mind, in perceiving, interacting, and engaging with the surrounding world. Simply stated, embodied learning involves being attentive to the body and its experiences as a way of knowing.

Experiencing Embodied Learning. Exploring experiences of embodied learning is useful for developing a deeper understanding of this phenomenon,

New Directions for Adult and Continuing Education • DOI: 10.1002/ace

particularly in regard to how to apply and integrate embodiment in learning contexts. As Colman (2003) notes, "Our experience is always embodied, always worldly, and always situated" (p. 4). With this in mind, most who discuss and research embodiment emphasize that embodiment is contextually based and involves social processes (Cheville, 1997, 2005; Colman, 2003; Freiler, 2007; Mills and Daniluk, 2002; Somerville, 2004). Accordingly, situated cognition is theoretically discussed as a way to understand how embodied learning emerges through the body's engagement in the process of activity and doing in situated experiences to construct knowledge (Fenwick, 2003; Michelson, 1998). This section explores several research-based and conceptual insights in these discussions in different learning contexts in the literature.

Beginning with research situating body-place relations as a way to understand experiences of embodied learning in the workplace, Somerville (2004) explores how miners learned workplace safety. Discussion of the miners' survival in a highly dangerous work setting focuses on embodied experiences in body-place relations in the mines "where one's survival depends on sensing minute changes in sounds, smell, feel of air" (Somerville, 2004, p. 60). The embodied knowledge of miners known as pit sense is the way in which miners inhabit their place in the mine and assess their safety while situated in the mine. This way of knowing hinges not only on keen sensory awareness of one's surroundings in a relationship with the mines but also on reliance on other miners inhabiting the same place in the mines. Somerville (2004) explains that pit sense "involves highly individual learning through the senses but at the same time an elevated sense of teamwork and trust where they depend for their lives on a team they will often not be able to see or hear" (p. 60).

There is a similar relational and situated understanding of embodied learning in research focusing on embodied experiences among women student athletes on an intercollegiate basketball team (Cheville, 1997, 2005). An understanding of how student athletes learn as athletes is present through bodily action and place as central units of analysis. These units also intersect with cultural influences in examining embodied learning within the context of team participation.

Similar to miners' pit sense, findings reveal that a court sense of place is manifest among players where they talk about relying on each other through a sense of being oriented to one another through bodily knowledge. The women student athletes describe their sense of embodied learning from collective body-place relations through bodily experiences and "the extent to which cultural place shapes bodily and conceptual orientation" (Cheville, 1997, p. 167). There is an apparent relational aspect of embodied learning through participatory team involvement that is considerably "linked to a sensitivity to otherness" (p. 59).

Drawing on insights of these researchers, I conducted an action research project integrating experiences of embodied learning in a higher education nursing class (Freiler, 2007). Examples of activities that I used to facilitate experiences of embodiment are attention to body awareness through a cultural lens while doing tai chi; focus on sensorimotor experience and sensory perception through diaphragmatic breathing, guided imagery, progressive muscle relaxation, yoga, and a "camp fire" guided visualization experience; attention to body inscriptions, delving into an awareness of how bodies are inscribed, marked, and scarred using critical incidents on body inscriptions and bodily experience of power differentials in bowing (Crowdes, 2000); focus on embodiment connected to creative expression, symbolic representation, and healing facilitated through music, dance, and artistic expression.

Participants in this project initially found embodiment difficult to verbally express as a concept, but they did develop a greater sense of understanding and meaning of how embodiment is conceptualized through experiential engagement and social processes. As experiences of embodied learning progressed throughout the semester, participants gave expression to a developed sense of embodied being-in-the-world. Visceral, emotive, and physiological connections of intensified embodied awareness were described by participants as "being in tune" to or with their bodies, "listening to" the body as it talks to them and tells them something, and "being more aware" of attending to body experiences and one's surroundings.

Other experiential activities in higher education interrelate embodied learning with affect in social processes to analyze power differentials in society manifested in racism, sexism, and classism (Crowdes, 2000) and social representations of racial consciousness (Yorks and Kasl, 2002). Crowdes (2000) discusses experiential activities in an undergraduate sociology course using a progressive bowing exercise with prescribed conditions of authority and submission. Learners experience and connect levels of cognitive, affective, and embodied responses for insight elicited from power differentials similar to those created by societal "-isms." Crowdes (2000) described the responses as "an integrity of mind, body, and action accompanied by some awareness of the nature of the connections in the broader social context" (p. 27). Yorks and Kasl (2002) also discuss experiential embodied engagement in a classroom context in terms of whole-person learning. From the context of "learning-within-relationship" (p. 177), adult learners participate in a collaborative inquiry process and experiential activity involving team presentations merging affective and cognitive domains of knowing with embodied representations to construct knowledge on themes of racial consciousness and racial identity. Learners construct presentations using physical positioning with various props, music, and movements to represent interaction styles and racial identity. Reflective descriptions of presentations from the teams capture the powerful depth of "felt encounter" (p. 179) experienced among learners from direct participation and observations. As a black team member notes,

"This clearly was a class assignment, yet the feelings we felt in our bodies were very real, alarming and validating at the same time" (pp. 178–179).

Other examples of experiences of embodied learning are visible in learning contexts related to improved quality of life and wellness (Beaudoin, 1999; Lord, 2002; Mills and Daniluk, 2002). Mills and Daniluk (2002), for example, investigate experiences of embodiment in exploring the lived experiences and meanings drawn from engagement in dance therapy for women dealing with issues of childhood sexual abuse, noting, "Indeed, the women in this study underscored the importance of being able to move 'out of their heads' and past their cognitive defenses, so that they could begin to attend to their bodily sensations, feelings, and impulses" (p. 85). Connecting emotions and bodily experience through dance movements facilitated profound change and healing for these women.

In other research investigating experiences of embodied learning, Lord (2002) explored embodied and somatic learning in relation to well-being. Lord's approach examined the potential positive impact of embodied and somatic learning on well-being in a university campus staff wellness program. Experiences in yoga, qigong, and other stress management techniques were implemented to focus on body awareness, breathing, flexibility, and spiritual dimensions of wellness.

In summary, what can be drawn from discussions on embodiment is that whether it occurs among villagers off the coast of Thailand, among adult learners in a higher education class, among miners deep in the bowels of a coal mine, among athletes on a basketball court, or among abused women in dance therapy, the conceptualization and experience of embodiment emerges within social processes in particular contexts. Experiences of embodied learning also demonstrate that embodiment is most readily accessed through the realm of subjectivity facilitated by direct, experiential engagement as an alternative way to construct knowledge.

Embodiment and Learning: Implications for Theory and Practice

As an alternative link to traditional practice enhancing significant learning experiences, embodiment is becoming established in the discourse with innovative developments in theory and practice. This section discusses the implications of embodied learning related to these developments.

Theoretical Implications. As the systematic study of adult learning seeks to explain how adults learn, attention to the body is emerging as a new direction. Theoretical discussions of embodiment are becoming associated with holistic frameworks and innovative practices that link bodies and minds through multiple ways of knowing with a shift in scholarly interest toward interrelated knowing processes (Clark, 2001; Grauerholz, 2001; Tisdell, 2003; Yang, 2003; Yorks and Kasl, 2002). From the vantage of exploring the value of embodied knowledge in adult learning, Clark (2001) discusses the significance of embodiment as an opportunity to open other spaces within educational contexts, to "encourage adult educators to look around and to notice new modes of learning" (p. 91), and to present crucial questions that direct and stimulate discussion on revaluing embodiment in learning.

Developments in revaluing and reconnecting minds and bodies are emerging in small circles of innovative approaches (Nikitina, 2003; Ross, 2000). Nikitina (2003) notes a need to search for "better ways to connect and explain the unity of mind and body" (p. 63) as essential to learning through integrative approaches crossing disciplines. Ross (2000) highlights the pedagogical value of integrating mind, body, and affect through a holistic paradigm in dance education in an academy context, noting that "the boundaries of academic disciplines are being rendered increasingly permeable" (Ross, 2000, p. 28). Tisdell's attention to spirituality and culture in learning (2003) discusses facilitating activities "honoring the various dimensions of how people learn and construct knowledge" (p. 194; for example, affective, somatic, symbolic, cognitive, spiritual, and cultural domains). These areas demonstrate that traditional boundaries of knowing are beginning to fade in favor of innovative approaches reconnecting mind and body.

Practical Implications. As an initial guideline, embodiment needs to be viewed within a broader movement toward holistic, integrative learning approaches wherein the body is made more visible as a source of knowledge and site for learning through objective and subjective realms of knowing. Embodiment warrants being approached from a multidimensional perspective given its complexity and more abstract nature as a concept and problem for practice. Thus, experiences of embodiment should focus on merging and balancing somatic dimensions of learning with other domains of knowing across multiple levels of knowledge construction.

Next, a multidimensional approach needs to take into account the personalized individual nature of approaching the body in learning along a continuum with social processes and sociocultural influences as intersecting units of analysis. The body's physical essence and the body as a site of learning need to be seen in conjunction with the sociocultural influences and social processes in effect through experiential engagement. Thus, approaching the body needs to comprehensively include intersecting theoretical orientations of learning.

Additionally, an embodied approach needs to be appropriately customized to the learning context given the relevance of contextual factors. This customization should be based on commonalities and differences among learners in considering how to incorporate appropriate experiences of embodiment. In previous studies, shared connections among learners was found to be highly important for fostering a sense of relatedness and

New Directions for Adult and Continuing Education • DOI: 10.1002/ace

comfort in approaching the body in learning (Freiler, 2007; Mills and Daniluk, 2002; Yorks and Kasl, 2002). The kinds of experiences provided also depend on the background and comfort level of the instructor or facilitator.

The relevance for bringing attention to the body within the learning context needs to be made explicit. Decisions need to be carefully weighed about when, where, and how to integrate experiences of embodiment to enhance learning. Some learners may view a holistic approach with disdain as poorly structured and not as relevant for learning (Grauerholz, 2001). The possibility of resistance and discomfort among learners needs to be closely monitored, given that some learners may prefer and expect a more traditional, rational approach to learning. Thus timing, relevance, and establishment of a comfortable space that affords support and choices for exploration in direct experience need to be sensitively navigated in learning spaces.

Most important, finding a comfortable way to approach and come to terms with body disconnect as a given for most learners is crucial. Approaching the body is highly personal and private in nature for most individuals. In summary, it can be arrived at by carefully providing choices and fostering a level a comfort for learners to directly participate in and reflect on experiences of embodiment in the immediate moment while leaving room for observation.

The value of embodied learning discussed in the literature as a significant, alternative way to gain and apply new knowledge outweighs the considerations, challenges, and complexities of how to approach embodiment. The learning community has been referred to as "spaces in which our bodies exist and profess" (Freedman and Holmes, 2003, p. 7). Learning occurs in social contexts and bodies, not just in minds. The evolving understanding of embodiment is beginning to remove the body from a place of otherness into practicing space where both body and mind are being more holistically approached and valued. Just as the Mokens survived the tsunami, our very survival may indeed one day depend on embodiment in our personal spaces as a way of knowing.

References

Beaudoin, C. "Integrating Somatic Learning into Everyday Life." *Canadian Journal of Education*, 1999, 24(1), 76–80.

Bermudez, J. L., Marcel, A., and Eilan, N. (eds.). *The Body and the Self*. Cambridge, Mass.: MIT Press, 1998.

Brockman, J. "A Somatic Epistemology for Education." *Educational Forum*, 2001, 65(4), 328–334.

Cheville, J. B. "Learning as Embodiment: Playing the Game." Dissertation Abstracts International, 58(8), 3188. UMI no. AAT9805653, 1997.

Cheville, J. B. "Confronting the Problem of Embodiment." *International Journal of Qualitative Studies in Education*, 2005, *8*(1), 85–107.

Clark, C. M. "Off the Beaten Path: Some Creative Approaches to Adult Learning—Somatic Learning and Narrative Learning." *New Directions for Adult and Continuing Education*, no. 89. San Francisco: Jossey-Bass, 2001.

Colman, A. V. "Subjectivity, Embodiment, and Meaning in Merleau-Ponty and Irigaray." Dissertation Abstracts International, *64*(10), 3708. UMI no. AAT3108553, 2003.

Crowdes, M. S. "Embodying Sociological Imagination: Pedagogical Support for Linking Bodies to Minds." *Teaching Sociology*, 2000, *28*(1), 24–40.

Csordas, T. J. (ed.). *Embodiment and Experience: The Existential Ground of Culture and Self*. New York: Cambridge University Press, 1994.

Damasio, A. R. *The Feeling of What Happens: Body and Emotion in the Making of Consciousness*. Orlando: Harcourt Brace, 1999.

Fenwick, T. "Reclaiming and Re-Embodying Experiential Learning Through Complexity Science." *Studies in the Education of Adults*, 2003, *35*(2), 123–141.

Freedman, D. P., and Holmes, M. S. (eds.). *The Teacher's Body: Embodiment, Authority, and Identity in the Academy*. Albany: State University of New York Press, 2003.

Freiler, T. J. "Bridging Traditional Boundaries of Knowing: Revaluing Mind/Body Connections Through Experiences of Embodiment." Unpublished doctoral dissertation, Department of Adult Education, Pennsylvania State University, 2007.

Grauerholz, E. "Teaching Holistically to Achieve Deep Learning." *College Teaching*, 2001, *49*(2), 44–50.

Lakoff, G., and Johnson, M. *Philosophy in the Flesh: The Embodied Mind and Its Challenge to Western Thought*. New York: Basic Books, 1999.

Lee, M., Lee, E., Lee, M., and Lee, J. *The Healing Art of Tai Chi*. New York: Sterling, 1996.

Lord, D. L. "Exploring the Role of Somatic Education in Experiential Well-Being." *Dissertation Abstracts International, 63*(04), 1269. UMI no. AAT3049078, 2002.

Merriam, S., Caffarella, R., and Baumgartner, L. *Learning in Adulthood*. San Francisco: Jossey-Bass, 2007.

Michelson, E. "Re-Membering: The Return of the Body to Experiential Learning." *Studies in Continuing Education*, 1998, *20*(2), 217–232.

Mills, L. J., and Daniluk, J. C. "Her Body Speaks: The Experience of Dance Therapy for Women Survivors of Child Sexual Abuse." *Journal of Counseling and Development*, 2002, *80*(1), 77–86.

Nikitina, S. "Movement Class as an Integrative Experience: Academic, Cognitive, and Social Effects." *Journal of Aesthetic Education*, 2003, *37*(1), 54–63.

Price, J., and Shildrick, M. (eds.). *Feminist Theory and the Body: A Reader*. New York: Routledge, 1999.

Ross, J. "Arts Education in the Information Age: A New Place for Somatic Wisdom." *Arts Education Policy Review*, 2000, *101*(6), 27–32.

Simon, B. (Producer). *60 Minutes* [television broadcast]. New York: CBS News, Mar. 20, 2005.

Simon, S. "Subjectivity and the Experiencing Body: Toward an Ecological Foundation for Adult Learning." Dissertation Abstracts International, *59*(08), 2900. UMI no. AAT9904058, 1998.

Somerville, M. "Tracing Bodylines: The Body in Feminist Poststructural Research." *International Journal of Qualitative Studies in Education*, 2004, *17*(1), 47–63.

Tisdell, E. *Exploring Spirituality and Culture in Adult and Higher Education*. San Francisco: Jossey-Bass, 2003.

Weiss, G., and Haber, H. F. (eds.). *Perspectives on Embodiment: The Intersections of Nature and Culture*. New York: Routledge, 1999.

Yang, B. "Toward a Holistic Theory of Knowledge and Adult Learning." *Human Resource Development Review*, 2003, 2(2), 106–129.

Yorks, L., and Kasl, E. "Toward a Theory and Practice for Whole-Person Learning: Reconceptualizing Experience and the Role of Affect." *Adult Education Quarterly*, 2002, 52(3), 176–192.

TAMMY J. FREILER is an educational specialist in secondary school counseling and an adjunct faculty member at the Pennsylvania State University and Alvernia College.

New Directions for Adult and Continuing Education • DOI: 10.1002/ace

5

The chapter examines how the brain uses experience as a basis for learning and how learning changes the brain.

Teaching with the Brain in Mind

Kathleen Taylor, Annalee Lamoreaux

> I would have the experience but . . . I left the learning *behind* somewhere. During the course, I realized that the learning really *was* there, I just never *accessed* it. . . . So once I started to realize, through writing the papers, that it was *there* . . . [I was] able to go internally and access it, and link it up with thinking. And I can actually use it now.
>
> —LM, a forty-eight-year-old Caucasian woman

> I started looking at myself and what was going on and in the world around. I just started looking at everything a little differently. . . . Where was I going? What was the point of certain things that I was doing? My job started becoming a real problem too . . . because when you start examining yourself, you examine the whole world around besides yourself.
>
> —JH, thirty-eight-year-old African American woman

As adult educators, we are committed to learning that encourages adults to see themselves and the world around them in more complex ways. We have therefore focused our practice on teaching with development in mind (Taylor, 2000; Lamoreaux, 2005). Recently, however, a colleague (Johnson, 2003) pointed us to a body of research that examines how the brain changes as it learns. We found it offered us a new and valuable perspective on teaching and learning. This chapter therefore describes aspects of brain function that suggest ways to teach with the brain in mind.

New Directions for Adult and Continuing Education, no. 119, Fall 2008 © 2008 Wiley Periodicals, Inc.
Published online in Wiley InterScience (www.interscience.wiley.com) • DOI: 10.1002/ace.305

The Essential Brain

The brain's task is to preserve the organism by monitoring what goes on in and around the body, such as blood pressure, heart rate, and glucose levels as well as all data coming in through the senses, in order to continuously make adjustments intended to keep the body safe and functioning effectively. When faced with danger, the survival response releases hormones that prepare the body to fight or flee. The pleasure response encourages reproduction, maternal care of infants, and consumption of high-calorie foods.

Though these internal responses are not under conscious control, we can learn to choose the resulting behaviors—which is just as crucial to our long-term survival. When, for instance, someone accidentally bumps into us, we can ignore the rush of adrenaline and calm down rather than fight or run. When offered a delicious fat-and-sugar confection, we can politely decline and perhaps go for a walk instead.

Though all other cells in the body are regularly replaced, we are born with most of the brain cells (neurons) we will have. Rather than replacement, neurons "get changed by learning . . . [which changes] the way they connect with others" (Damasio, 1999, p. 144). Barring injury, disease, or the eventual breakdown that occurs as cell replacement slows with age, other organs continue to function as usual. Learning, however, changes how the brain functions, increasing our capacity for innovative, flexible responses to external conditions.

Anatomy and Memory. Memory enables individuals to reconsider previous experience when dealing in the present or planning for the future. To explain, we will greatly simplify the anatomy of a neuron.

Imagine a child's sketch of a tree: roots, thick base, slender trunk, and leafy branches. In the brain, an electrochemical signal starts at the "roots" (dendrites), flows to the "base" (cell body), up the "trunk" (axon), and then to the "branches" (axon terminals). The signal then passes across a space (synapse) from one of the branches to the roots or base of another tree, creating a web of interconnections. "When the organism is exposed to a new pattern of signals from the outside world, the strengths of the synaptic contacts (the ease of signal passage between neurons) . . . gradually change" leading to more complex connections throughout the brain; *"this represents learning as we understand it today"* (Goldberg, 2001, p. 29, italics added). Repeatedly activated connections become stronger; they "fire together, [therefore] wire together." They also grow "bushier" dendrites, leading to more connections that may shrink synaptic spaces, resulting in a more tightly woven pattern of neurons (Goldberg, 2001; Siegel, 1999). By contrast, fewer follow-up experiences may lead to looser connections. Thus experience leads to changes in neural networks throughout the brain, including how information is "encoded."

This encoding is not typically what we think of when referring to "a memory," however; rather than being something stored in a particular *place* in the brain, memory is a *process*.

> Memories are *constructions assembled* [from various places in the brain] *at the time of retrieval*, and the information stored during the initial experience is only one of the items used in the construction; other contributions include information already stored in the brain, as well as things the person hears or sees and then stores after the experience. [LeDoux, 2002, p. 203; italics added].

What comes into conscious awareness is therefore affected by the individual's filters or frames of reference: "Memory is modified each time it is remembered" (Cozolino, 2002, p. 103).

When storing new sensory input, the brain "looks for" connections to earlier information. New data that can be related to existing patterns appear to "make sense" and are therefore more likely to be remembered. But confronted with ideas for which their brains can find no related prior experience, and therefore no meaningful links to existing patterns, learners may find them difficult to retain. If adults are further stressed as by an impending exam, rather than working to create new connections they may try to memorize—"knowledge" that, as educators know, rarely lasts.

Complexity of Mind. The brain uses analogy to connect new input to existing patterns: How is the current experience like some earlier experience? Being able to use the past to evaluate present situations is an evolutionary advantage that no doubt came in very handy each subsequent time our cave-dwelling ancestors faced things with fangs and claws. Even more significant, the brain's "rules" (algorithm) for analyzing connections between new and old patterns become more complex over our lifetime. The phenomenal power of the human mind derives in large part from the fact that the brain learns to change its own algorithm to account for variations, contrasts, and more integrative metaphors, leading to more inclusive, creative, and flexible responses to unfolding experience (Cozolino, 2002).

For example, consider changes over the lifespan in how people make sense of others' needs. A toddler will often grab something from a playmate, insisting it is "mine." School-aged children can usually be induced to share, even if unwillingly. By late adolescence, some young adults respond to their peers' needs or desires without sufficient regard for their own well-being. A mature adult, however, is likely to examine the situation from various perspectives and choose actions in keeping with his or her value system. Unfortunately, these capacities—for objective analysis of both situation and self—are not evenly developed among adults (Kegan, 1994).

Take the effectiveness of phrases such as "cut and run" or "stay and pay" in forming public opinion about the Iraq war. By triggering existing neural networks, these superficial analogies can evoke in many adults predictable responses that are not conscious, hence unavailable for reflection. A primary task for adult educators may therefore be to create learning environments that encourage adults' brains to be less susceptible to such manipulation. Learners who can recognize the speaker's intentions and also examine their own assumptions have developed capacities that Mezirow and associates (2000) relate to "liberated person[s]" who are better able to take charge of their own lives (p. 26).

Plasticity. Plasticity refers to the brain's capacity to "rewire" or modify existing neural networks.

> The growth and connectivity of neurons is the basic mechanism of all learning and adaptation. Learning can be reflected in neural changes in a number of ways, including the growth of new neurons, the expansion of existing neurons, and changes in the connectivity between existing neurons. All of these changes are expressions of plasticity, or the ability of the nervous system to change [Cozolino, 2002, p. 20].

Children's brains are extremely plastic, to allow adaptation to their environment. Though the plasticity of adults' brains diminishes with age, some losses are compensated by gains from the elaboration of neural networks generated by more experience (Siegel, 1999).

Meaning Making and Constructing Knowledge

At the cellular level, learning is about creating lasting neural patterns that can be effectively accessed. But this could apply to rote learning, skill development, or stimulus-reward behavioral training. As described earlier, our intentions for our adult learners go beyond mastering behavioral skills or informational content. We focus on what we consider meta-objectives of adult higher education, such as "the understanding that knowledge is neither given nor gotten, but constructed; the ability to take perspective on one's own beliefs; and the realization that learning and development are worthy life-long goals" (Taylor and Marienau, 1997, p. 233). This accords with Langer's definition of *mindful learning*: "the continuous creation of new categories; openness to new information; and an implicit awareness of more than one perspective" (1997, p. 4).

Adults who develop these more complex capacities are also likely to respond more effectively to what Kegan (1994, 2000) describes as the demands of modernity. For example, changing family structures require new ways of thinking about gender-related roles as well as what constitutes healthy partnerships, appropriate communication, and wise parenting. In the social milieu, increasing diversity calls for openness to others' ideas and beliefs, even when they are startlingly different from one's own. In many workplaces and educational settings, employees and learners are increasingly expected to question institutional assumptions as well as demonstrate greater capacity for critical self-reflection.

Developmental intentions also accord with the constructivist notion that meaning is made in the mind-brain of the learner, rather than merely received from the mind-brain of the teacher or author of the text. This is not to discount the social elements of meaning construction (Vygotsky, 1978), but rather to acknowledge that "though there is an indispensable social aspect to the construction of meaning, there is also an irreducible individual element" (Caine and Caine, 2006, p. 54).

Learning, Teaching, and the Brain

There is no one right way to teach adults. Nevertheless, student learning may be enhanced if educators align practice with how the brain functions (Cozolino, 2002; Johnson and Taylor, 2006; Zull, 2002). For example, the steps of Kolb's learning cycle (1984)—*concrete experience, reflective observation, abstract conceptualization,* and *active experimentation*—parallel how signals flow in the brain, from sensory input through various integrative functions to finally result in motor output. Zull (2002) terms these steps *experience, reflection, abstraction,* and *testing* and identifies them as the "four pillars of learning" (pp. 14–18).

Experience. For the brain to notice something, it must respond to signals traveling along nerve cells. Initially, however, "experiences don't happen to us, events happen to us" (Brookfield, 1998, p. 129). Sensory data are events that the brain turns into experience. Events are filtered physically (the brain cannot process all the simultaneous stimuli) and psychologically (we unconsciously choose which data we will attend to on the basis of sociocultural and other prior experiences). The brain's physical responses to the sensory data are recorded—literally, embodied—as experience, hence accessible to reconstruction as memory; without such physical responses, there is no basis for constructing meaning (Sheckley and Bell, 2006).

Current and prior experiences interact when new activities are unconsciously filtered through what the learner already "knows"—or thinks she does, which can lead to misinterpretation. Given that adults usually have some experience related, however tenuously, to course content, it is important that educators give these learners opportunities to make conscious connections.

For example, as experts in our fields most of us tend to introduce new material by framing it as we best understand it. In a course on adult development, we might provide an overview of various theories as they emerged in the latter part of the twentieth century, thus—we believe—laying a foundation for students to later read and analyze several theoretical viewpoints.

Another approach, however—one more likely to build on embodied experience—could first ask a diverse group of adults to individually note down significant personal and social milestones in each of their lives. Then, in small groups organized by age and gender, they could look for similarities and differences in these life-patterns. Finally, all the groups' discoveries would be synthesized, illuminating patterns of changes in gender- and age-related roles over time. When this group of learners then turns to the readings, their conscious connection to the theories can make subsequent analysis more meaningful. Zull (2002) is explicit: "A teacher must start with the existing networks of neurons in a learner's brain, because they are the physical form of her prior knowledge" (p. 8).

Listening to lectures and reading texts are valuable learning experiences, but the learners likely to derive the most benefit are those who can also draw on related prior experience. Caine and Caine (2006) explain: "More than reading is needed to make adequate sense of what is being read. At some stage, there is a need for physical and sensory participation or recall of sensory and physical events if full meaning is to emerge" (p. 55).

This suggests that offering concrete examples, analogies, and experiential activities, thus helping learners create meaningful connection, is—from the brain's perspective—a more effective approach to teaching and learning than focusing primarily on how we, as educators and experts, understand the issue.

Reflection. Reflection begins with the brain's association between new and past events, a physical process of searching for connections that leads to assembling and categorizing richer, more meaningful images and eventually, more complex neural networks (Zull, 2002). Reflection is therefore a key to *reframing*—that is, to reinterpreting past experiences in light of newer ones—because it can alter neural connections and therefore the meaning we make on the basis of those connections.

When new experiences do not readily fit existing patterns—an unsettling experience Mezirow (1990) calls a *disorienting dilemma*—the brain has an opportunity to forge new connections and therefore make new meaning that is "inclusive, discriminating, and integrative of experience [as well as open] to alternative perspectives" (p. 156). In their analysis of the importance of reflection to learning, Boud, Keogh, and Walker (1985) appear to have anticipated current understandings of brain function:

> Why is it that conscious reflection is necessary? Why can it not occur effectively at the unconscious level? . . . [Because] unconscious processes do not allow us to make active and aware decisions about our learning. It is only when we bring our ideas to our consciousness that we can evaluate them and begin to make choices about what we will and will not do [p. 19].

From a practitioner's perspective, journaling is an effective way to encourage reflection. Walden (1995) describes various low-stress assignments designed for adult learners unaccustomed to self-reflection in an academic setting.

We consider self-assessment as a specialized form of journaling. According to MacGregor (1993), potential outcomes for self-assessment include adults seeing "learning as a transaction between self and world . . . [which strengthens] their capacity to see themselves as agents of effective action" (p. 11). Boud, however, sees self-assessment as "a range of different practices in which learners take responsibility for making their own judgments about their work" (Taylor, Marienau, and Fiddler, 2000, p. 64).

In our practice, we tend to downplay the evaluative and judgment aspects of self-assessment and focus instead on asking adults to examine their *process* of learning itself—how they are engaging with the content, with one another, and with the various assignments. A journal entry reveals what can happen when adults reflect not just on course content but also on who they have been (and perhaps, are becoming) as learners:

> Are truths absolute? Are values situational? Should one ever question the church . . . ? Even more controversial, is it a sin to question God? In the few short weeks that I have been in this class I have come to ask myself these questions. There was a time when asking these types of questions was taboo for me. Even if the only place these questions were being asked was in the mind. Today, I am not as threatened by these thoughts. In fact, I believe that these thoughts will enlighten me and strengthen my beliefs, even though some of my beliefs may change [JC, a forty-two-year-old Hispanic man].

Over time, we find such reflections foster in adults greater competence and self-confidence in dealing with their strengths and weaknesses, and therefore more effective learning. For Zull (2002), "The art of directing and supporting reflection is part of the art of changing a brain . . . [and] leading a student toward comprehension" (p. 164).

Abstraction. Zull (2002) terms this *creating* and includes planning and problem solving. Such activities occur in the most recently evolved part of the brain: the front cortex or "executive brain" (Goldberg, 2001). These processes—making sense of things, solving problems, and deciding on courses of action—go on continuously—entirely unrelated to formal learning. We human beings make meaning as easily as we breathe—and we perish in the absence of either.

> Meaning is, in its origins, a physical activity (grasping, seeing), a social activity (it requires another), a survival activity (in doing it, we live). Meaning, understood in this way, is the primary human motion, irreducible. It cannot be divorced from the body, from social experience, or from the very survival of the organism [Kegan, 1982, pp. 18–19].

New Directions for Adult and Continuing Education • DOI: 10.1002/ace

But requiring learners to make conscious meaning on demand is a different sort of task, and one that involves both emotion and cognition. The cognitive activity includes manipulating and categorizing information in both long-term storage and working memory as well as relating between them, thus elaborating existing neural networks. The role of emotion, according to Damasio (1999), appears to be "a support system without which the edifice of reason cannot operate properly" (p. 42).

The tasks and assignments most supportive of abstract, creative thinking are, like real-life problems, "ill-structured" (Schön, 1983). Grappling with ambiguous problems depends on an integrative brain process that Goldberg (2001) calls *adaptive decision making*, which requires examining issues from multiple perspectives: "Resolving ambiguity . . . depends on my priorities at the moment, which may change depending on the context. . . . Very different [cognitive] processes [are] involved in solving strictly deterministic situations" (pp. 78–79).

In contrast to adaptive decision making, tasks such as solving deterministic or veridical problems (those with clear right-and-wrong answers), taking tests that assess short-term memory, and writing papers that focus on repeating what experts have said lead to much less complex meaning construction.

> In school we are given a problem and must find the correct answer. Only one
> correct answer usually exists. The answer is hidden. The question is clear-cut.
> But most real-life situations, outside of the narrow realm of technical prob-
> lems, are inherently ambiguous. The answer is hidden, and so is the question.
> Our purposes in life are general and vague [Goldberg, 2001, p. 77].

In general, the "best way to help students develop and engage their executive [brain] functions is to adopt a constructivist approach to teaching and learning" (Caine and Caine, 2006, p. 57). When learners are challenged to make meaning—which is at the heart of constructivist practice—their brains are stimulated differently than when they are asked to focus on meaning already made.

Testing

Putting new meaning to the test can reveal that the brain's process of association and categorization was inadequate or faulty. Ideally, this discovery becomes the starting point for another turn of the learning cycle leading toward clarification and correction.

> Converting [an image] into the precise form required for language helps us
> see the details in our image, or it makes us invent those details . . . and we
> may notice that something is missing, a gap in our thought that we would

never have seen without converting our abstraction into [testable] form [Zull, 2002, p. 208].

"Testing" in this context does not refer to exams, which create such anxiety in most adults that they may inhibit neural connections. Moreover, the most prevalent type, multiple-choice, gives learners little support in identifying or revising flaws in their thinking. Far better are assignments that involve synthesizing ideas learned at different times during a course (or program), working and thinking with other learners, and (as Sheckley and Bell, 2006, have done) situating course activities in settings other than the classroom.

Dialogue is also an effective tool for examining one's meaning making. A learner who reads actively, with her own thoughts in mind, is in dialogue with the text. Journals or self-assessments written with explicit attention to multiple perspectives (Walden, 1995) enable a learner to dialogue with the self. Dialogue with classmates (or, for that matter, anyone who wants to listen and talk about what is being learned) as well as the more formal interaction Mezirow (2000) calls *discourse* are yet another opportunity. Finally, formative feedback, a form of dialogue in which an educator both affirms and questions the learner's presentation of her ideas, also encourages learners to examine and possibly revise their thinking.

Role of the Adult Educator

Adult educators who want to teach with learners' brains in mind need also to recognize the emotional context of learning and therefore seek the most effective balance of support and challenge.

When mature, often-accomplished learners describe youthful experiences of deep shame following a schoolteacher's comments, it is evident that such emotions can inhibit learning well into adulthood. A high level of hormones associated with trauma and the survival response can negatively affect both memory and learning (Perry, 2006).

Furthermore, many adults are returning learners precisely because they were not able to complete their degrees earlier. Even those who had rewarding learning experiences as children may fear academic failure or have anxiety about their skills (Perry, 2006). They are further challenged if the learning on which they will be assessed dismisses their maturity, knowledge, and experience, relying instead primarily on their ability to absorb printed and lectured material. Though too much stress greatly inhibits learning, insufficient challenge can also have a negative impact; a bored brain stops attending.

The most successful learning environments from the perspective of developmental intentions are those that provide high support *and* high challenge (Daloz, 1987). Scaffolding is an effective strategy that offers both.

A scaffold is a temporary structure that enables builders to work beyond a level that is mostly formed in order to start construction of the next, higher level. Similarly, when adult learners construct new meaning, scaffolding enables them to operate beyond their certainties, at what Daloz calls their *growing edge*. The combination of high support and high challenge may be the "optimal" stress that enhances production of dendrites, which are the parts of neurons most responsible for the "connectedness" of neuronal patterns (Cozolino, 2002).

Conclusion

Until recently, philosophy was the primary way to explain *mind*, anatomy and physiology to explain *brain*, and psychology to explain *self*. Now that we can observe the brains of living persons, these understandings have begun to converge. Current brain imaging techniques reveal not only the architecture of the brain but how its functions create "thought," "personality," and "consciousness"—and how the brain changes itself. Though this research is still in its infancy, we feel it offers powerful support to educators who wish to facilitate the particular changes in the brain called learning.

References

Boud, D., Keogh, R., and Walker, D. (eds.). *Reflection: Turning Experience into Learning.* London: Kogan Page, 1985.

Brookfield, S. "Against Naïve Romanticism: From Celebration to the Critical Analysis of Experience." *Studies in Continuing Education*, 1998.

Caine, G., and Caine, R. "Meaningful Learning and the Executive Functions of the Brain." In S. Johnson and K. Taylor (eds.), *The Neuroscience of Adult Learning*. New Directions for Adult and Continuing Education, no. 110. San Francisco: Jossey-Bass, 2006.

Cozolino, L. *The Neuroscience of Psychotherapy: Building and Rebuilding the Human Brain.* New York: Norton, 2002.

Daloz, L. *Effective Teaching and Mentoring.* San Francisco: Jossey-Bass, 1987.

Damasio, A. *The Feeling of What Happens: Body and Emotion in the Making of Consciousness.* Orlando: Harcourt Brace, 1999.

Goldberg, E. *The Executive Brain: Frontal Lobes and the Civilized Mind.* New York: Oxford University Press, 2001.

Johnson, S. "Facilitating the 'Self' of Adult Learners Moving Through Mid-Life Transition." Doctoral dissertation, Walden University, 2003. *Digital Dissertations*, AAT3095120.

Johnson, S., and Taylor, K. (eds.) *The Neurophysiology of Adult Learning.* New Directions for Adult and Continuing Education, no. 110. San Francisco: Jossey-Bass, 2006.

Kegan, R. *The Evolving Self.* Cambridge, Mass.: Harvard University Press, 1982.

Kegan, R. *In over Our Heads: The Mental Demands of Modern Life.* Cambridge, Mass.: Harvard University Press, 1994.

Kegan, R. "What Form Transforms? A Constructive-Developmental Approach to Transformational Learning." In J. Mezirow and Associates (eds.), *Learning as Transformation.* San Francisco: Jossey-Bass, 2000.

Kolb, D. A. *Experiential Learning: Experience as the Source of Learning and Development*. Upper Saddle River, N.J.: Prentice-Hall, 1984.

Lamoreaux, A. "Adult Learners' Experience of Change Related to Prior Learning Assessment." Doctoral dissertation, Walden University, 2005. Digital Dissertations AAT3180108.

Langer, E. J. *The Power of Mindful Learning*. Cambridge, Mass.: Da Capo Press, 1997.

LeDoux, J. *The Synaptic Self: How Our Brains Become Who We Are*. New York: Penguin Books, 2002.

MacGregor, J. (ed.) *Student Self-Evaluation: Fostering Reflective Learning*. New Directions for Teaching and Learning, no. 56. San Francisco: Jossey-Bass, 1993.

Mezirow, J. *Transformative Dimensions of Adult Learning*. San Francisco: Jossey-Bass, 1990.

Mezirow, J., and Associates. *Learning as Transformation*. San Francisco: Jossey-Bass, 2000.

Perry, B. "Fear and Learning: Trauma-Related Factors in the Adult Education Process." In S. Johnson and K. Taylor (eds.), *The Neuroscience of Adult Learning*. New Directions for Adult and Continuing Education, no. 110. San Francisco: Jossey-Bass, 2006.

Sheckley, B., and Bell, S. "Experience, Consciousness, and Learning: Implications for Instruction." In S. Johnson and K. Taylor (eds.), *The Neuroscience of Adult Learning*. New Directions for Adult and Continuing Education, no. 110. San Francisco: Jossey-Bass, 2006.

Schön, D. *The Reflective Practitioner: How Professionals Think in Action*. New York: Basic Books, 1983.

Siegel, D. *The Developing Mind*. New York: Guilford Press, 1999.

Taylor, K. "Teaching with Developmental Intention." In J. Mezirow and Associates (eds.), *Learning as Transformation*. San Francisco: Jossey-Bass, 2000.

Taylor, K., and Marienau, C. "Constructive-Development Theory as a Framework for Assessment in Higher Education." *Assessment and Evaluation in Higher Education*, 1997, 22(2), 233–243.

Taylor, K., Marienau, C., and Fiddler, M. *Developing Adult Learners: Strategies for Teachers and Trainers*. San Francisco: Jossey-Bass, 2000.

Vygotsky, L. *Mind in Society: The Development of Higher Psychological Processes*. Cambridge, Mass.: Harvard University Press, 1978.

Walden, P. "Journal Writing: A Tool for Women Developing as Knowers." In K. Taylor and C. Marienau (eds.), *Learning Environments for Women's Adult Development: Bridges Toward Change*. New Directions for Adult and Continuing Education, no. 65. San Francisco: Jossey-Bass, 1995.

Zull, J. E. *The Art of Changing the Brain*. Sterling, Va.: Stylus, 2002.

KATHLEEN TAYLOR *is professor in the graduate Educational Leadership Program, Kalmanovitz School of Education, Saint Mary's College of California.*

ANNALEE LAMOREAUX *is chair, prior learning assessment and adult development, Saint Mary's College of California.*

6

Narrative is not only a method for fostering learning; it is also a way to conceptualize the learning process. In this chapter, we describe the essential features of narrative learning and discuss why this is such an effective way to teach adults.

Narrative Learning in Adulthood

M. Carolyn Clark, Marsha Rossiter

Narrative is on the move. Actually it's been on the move for some time, but education, and more specifically adult education, has only begun catching the wave relatively recently. Of course, using stories to teach has always been part of the practice of adult educators. What is more recent is the theorizing of how we learn through narrative (Clark, 2001; Rossiter and Clark, 2007), but even that has deep connections to the core elements of adult learning theory, as we'll see. Our task in this chapter is to examine what narrative learning is, how it works, and how it can be used more intentionally and effectively in the education of adults. We hope to stimulate further conversation and thought about the possibilities inherent in conceptualizing learning as a narrative process. We begin with an overview of narrative theory, examine the connection between experiential and narrative learning, and follow that with a description of what we mean by narrative learning and how learning itself can be conceptualized as a narrative process. We then look at several examples of narrative learning in practice and conclude with some thoughts about the potential of narrative learning theory for the field of adult education.

Fundamentals of Narrative Theory for Narrative Learning

Human beings are the creatures who tell stories—a point Fisher (1987) makes when he gives us the label *homo narrans*—and those stories serve a function, namely to make meaning of our experience. This basic idea has been developed by a number of theorists in recent decades (for example,

New Directions for Adult and Continuing Education, no. 119, Fall 2008 © 2008 Wiley Periodicals, Inc.
Published online in Wiley InterScience (www.interscience.wiley.com) • DOI: 10.1002/ace.306

Cohere

Polkinghorne, 1988; Bruner, 1990; Irwin, 1996; Sarbin, 1986) who argue that meaning making is a narrative process. This makes sense at a very basic level. Everyday we are bombarded by a dizzying variety of experiences and we make sense of those by storying them, by constructing narratives that make things cohere. Coherence creates sense out of chaos by establishing connections between and among these experiences. Sometimes it's a matter of locating experiences within a particular cultural narrative, for example recognizing that advertising is part of the cultural narrative of consumption and is not just a bid for us to buy particular products. This recognition also makes possible the critique of that cultural narrative and offers the possibility for development of a counter narrative; with respect to advertising, for example, a counter narrative is the anticonsumption message of the simple living movement. At other times it's a matter of constructing a narrative for ourselves that enables us to deal with an experience. An example here would be responding to an illness by constructing a narrative of restoration and hope, as opposed to a narrative of victimization, struggle, or loss. The choice of narrative—the sense we make of an experience—determines how we respond to and manage that experience.

Narrative is also how we craft our sense of self, our identity. Rosenwald and Ochberg (1992, p. 1) argue, "Personal stories are not merely a way of telling someone (or oneself) about one's life; they are the means by which identities may be fashioned." McAdams (1985) works from a similar premise in his life story model of identity in which the self is understood as an ever-unfolding story. We story our identities in multiple and sometimes contradictory ways; in one context we can see ourselves as the hero of the story, while in another we are someone whose agency is limited. These multiple narratives that constitute our identity enable us to manage the complexity of who we are. Understanding identity as a narrative construction is another way of conceptualizing personal change. Kenyon and Randall (1997) think of this process as restorying our lives, which is to say that when a story of the self no longer coheres, no longer helps us make sense of our experience, then we must change it. Randall (1996) in fact describes transformative learning as a process of restorying.

Closely related to the understanding of identity itself as an unfolding story is, of course, the narrative orientation to lifespan development. People understand not only themselves but also the changes over the course of their lives narratively. A narrative approach to development, in contrast with other theoretical orientations, attempts to describe development from the inside as it is experienced, rather than from the outside as it is observed (Rossiter, 1999). The focus is on subjective meaning: how people make sense of their experiences over the life course. In this view, construction of an acceptable life narrative is the central process of adult development. The life narrative is repeatedly revised and enlarged throughout one's life to accommodate new insights, events, and perspectives. Developmental change is experienced and assessed through this process of storying and restorying one's life. As one moves into midlife from young adulthood, for example, one advances the plot of the life narrative accordingly, sees oneself in a new role, and understands the developmental change in relation to the similar passages of others in one's social or family groups. The stories of significant transitions throughout life, such as landing a first job, losing a parent, coping with major illness, or retiring from a career, when considered collectively express the meaning one makes of developmental growth throughout one's life. According to Cohler (1982), narrative may offer a better understanding of the life course than stage theory because it closely parallels the storying process that people use in making meaning of their own lives. A key feature of narrative development is that it defines development according to the interpretations of the developing person. Freeman (1991) describes this as an ongoing process of "rewriting the self" and argues that it is fundamentally retrospective. He says, "It is only after one has arrived at what is arguably or demonstrably a better psychological place than where one has been before that development can be said to have occurred" (p. 99).

It is also important to recognize that construction of a narrative is not purely a personal process; it is also social in nature. We live in what Sarbin (1993) calls "a story-shaped world" (p. 63), surrounded by narratives of all kinds that embody our cultural values—popular movies and television shows, myths and folklore, religious histories and traditions, social scripts and mores, to note only a few—and that all of these provide "libraries of plots . . . [that] help us interpret our own and other people's experience" (p. 59). Linde (1993) makes this point in another way, noting that we construct our narratives by drawing on a cultural supply of normal events, reasonable causes, and plausible explanations and that these cultural elements confer legitimacy on our narratives. The other social aspect of personal narratives is that they require an audience, an Other either real or imagined that responds to the narrative in some way; in this sense these narratives are performances of identity, played out in various ways but always shaped by cultural norms.

Narrative learning falls under the larger category of constructivist learning theory, which understands learning as construction of meaning from experience. The fundamental principles of narrative underlie this type of learning because the meaning construction is done narratively. Experiential learning theory also informs narrative learning; experience is the object of the meaning making. We turn now to a discussion of this connection.

Connections Between Experiential and Narrative Learning

Learning in adulthood is integrally related to lived experience. The relationship is understood in various ways by theorists of experiential learning

(Fenwick, 2000, 2004; Merriam, Caffarella, and Baumgartner, 2007) but has been a theme running through the literature since the earliest conceptions of adult learning. In the 1920s, Lindeman drew on the work of Dewey to advocate for adult education structured around the life world of the adult learner because this is the source of the adult's motivation to learn. His claim that "experience is the adult's living textbook" (Lindeman, 1961, p. 121) has served as a mantra for experience-based adult education for nearly a century. Equally well-known, of course, is Knowles's conception of andragogy (1980) in which experience has a prominent role. A main assumption of andragogy is that adults bring a store of life experience to the learning encounter and experience can serve as a resource for learning. Knowles called for more participatory methods that draw on the adult learners' lived experience in the educational setting.

In the development of adult learning theory, experience plays a central role, but there are several ways in which experience and learners are understood to be connected, and associated with conceptualizations of where the learning is located. In constructivist learning theory, learners connect to their experience through reflection on that experience, and learning is located in reflection. The nature of the reflection process varies—happening after the experience (Kolb, 1984), in the midst of the experience, as well as afterwards (Boud and Walker (1990), and taking in not just the experience but also underlying premises and assumptions (Mezirow, 1991; Mezirow and Associates, 2000). Fenwick (2004) argues that constructivists presume the person and his or her experiences exist separate from one another. In situated learning theory, learning happens in the interaction between learners and their contexts; reflection is not erased, but it occurs within this social and highly contextual interaction. Lave and Wenger (1991) argue that adults learn by working together within a community, using tools that are part of the community. This learning is highly pragmatic and deeply embedded within a social context, and in fact it is the form of learning most common to our everyday experience (Hansman, 2001). In narrative learning theory, we argue that there is an even closer connection between learners and experience. The nature of experience is always prelinguistic; it is "languaged" after the fact, and the process of narrating it is how learners give meaning to experience. Narrative learning is constructivist in character, but the construction of the narrative is necessary to make the experience accessible (that is, to language it), and how it is constructed determines what meaning it has for the person. To help clarify these connections, we turn now to a discussion of the nature of narrative learning.

Narrative Learning

Working from the premise that narrative is a uniquely human way of meaning making, we believe narrative learning is a twofold concept: fostering learning through stories, and conceptualizing the learning process itself. We consider these aspects separately.

Learning Through Stories. As we noted at the beginning of this chapter, using stories to foster learning is anything but new. Learning through stories is a multifaceted process. Most simply, it involves stories heard, stories told, and stories recognized. First, the *hearing* of stories implies reception; the stories come from outside the learner and must be received and interpreted by the learner. Stories are powerful precisely because they engage learners at a deeply human level. Stories draw us into an experience at more than a cognitive level; they engage our spirit, our imagination, our heart, and this engagement is complex and holistic. Good stories transport us away from the present moment, sometimes even to another level of consciousness. They evoke other experiences we've had, and those experiences become real again. A particularly moving example of this is stories told at a funeral about the person who has died; the stories are powerful because they make the person present again, and that presence is relational, speaking to the connections all of us make with others and how significant those connections are.

Second is the *telling* of stories, and now the learner is the actor rather than the receiver. In the classroom context, this means the learner moves from a cognitive understanding of a concept to link it to his or her own experience. But this does not simply mean the learner has plucked an example of this concept from a collection of personal experiences; it means the learner has made a connection between the two, and in the making of the connection new learning occurs. The course content now is also more real and personal and immediate, which in turn makes the engagement the learner has with the content more complex; more is involved than mere cognitive understanding. The learner is more connected to the course because of a personal contribution to it. An example here is when students in a course on adult learning share stories of transformative learning experiences; in the telling they not only recreate those experiences but do so from within a theoretical framework about this type of learning. This positioning enables them to understand their experiences of transformative learning in a new way.

The third element, *recognizing* stories, is more abstract. It presumes that learners begin to understand the fundamental narrative character of experience. As they gain understanding, they also begin to understand that they themselves are narratively constituted and narratively positioned; this applies to themselves personally, as well as to groups, societies, and cultures. One example would be Americans recognizing they are positioned within a particular cultural narrative, one that privileges the individual over the community and emphasizes rights more than responsibilities; by recognizing this narrative situatedness, American learners could critique this larger narrative, question underlying assumptions and inherent power relationships, and identify whose interests are served and whose are exploited by this narrative. This level of learning through stories connects with critical pedagogy and its emancipatory possibilities.

So, how is this layered notion of learning through stories related to the core tradition of experiential learning in adult education? We believe narrative learning builds on this tradition and extends it. Narrative links learning to the prior experience of the learner, but at a profoundly human level. It is constructivist, but it involves more than reflection on experience. It is situated, but in way that differs from the practical, problem-solving character of situated cognition. It is critical in that it enables learners to question and critique social norms and power arrangements, but it does so by enabling learners to see how they are located in (and their thinking is shaped by) larger cultural narratives. We believe narrative learning opens us as educators and as learners to greater possibilities.

Conceptualizing Learning as a Narrative Process. Narrative learning also offers us a new way to think about how learning occurs. We said at the beginning of this chapter that meaning making is a narrative process, and meaning making is the constructivist definition of learning. When we're learning something, what we're essentially doing is trying to make sense of it, discern its internal logic, and figure out how it's related to what we know already. The way we do this is by creating a narrative about what we're learning; in other words, we work to story it, to make the elements of what we do not yet fully understand hang together. We work to achieve coherence. We can do it in our heads, we can do it out loud, we can do it on paper, and it can be done alone or with others. The process of constructing the narrative, the story, is how we can see our understanding of something come together and make sense. It's a complex process in which we identify and struggle with the pieces we cannot make fit together (that is, what we do not understand yet), and we see the gaps (what we still do not know); seeing both helps us keep working on the construction of the narrative until finally it begins to hold together and make sense. Those of us who have lived abroad for any period of time experience this vividly—the shock of the new culture gradually subsides as we learn how to make our way in this new context. We construct a narrative of what was at first strange now becoming familiar, of values and ways of being in the world slowly making sense to us who are outsiders to the culture. It's a continuous process, of course; narratives like this are always tentative and evolving, which is appropriate because learning itself has no endpoint. But this narrative construction, this storying of our growing understanding of something, is how we make our learning visible to ourselves. What we're arguing here is that constructing a coherent narrative is how, in fact, we learn.

This concept of learning is something we commonly experience in practice. When we try to teach someone something for the first time, we know the truth of the common saying, "To teach something is to learn twice." Before we can teach anything, it must first make sense to us in some way, but putting our understanding in words that make sense to someone else—in other words, narrating it—furthers our own understanding of the subject. This is illustrated by the increasingly popular strategy of peer teaching (Brady, Holt, and Welt, 2003; Rubin and Hebert, 1998). When one student teaches a concept to another student, not only does the peer teacher benefit by creating the narrative but there is the further benefit that comes from having the student learner question or challenge the narrative. Those questions force the peer teacher to refine and develop the narrative, which is to say that the peer teacher learns in the very act of teaching. A similar thing happens when we write. Writing is a way of making our thinking visible, and we believe this becomes part of the thought process itself—thinking on paper—because we are trying to narrate our understanding of something, trying to achieve coherence. It's a powerful tool for learning.

Narrative Learning in Practice

Here we present three modes of narrative learning: learning journals, concept-focused autobiographical writing, and instructional case studies. In each case we examine how the learning is accomplished narratively.

Learning Journals. All the characteristics of narrative learning are caught up in the writing of learning journals. In this assignment, students are asked to articulate what they are learning in a course and to do so in a sustained, regular way. It is this sustained element of journaling that creates the opportunity for students to watch their understanding of the topic grow over time. Because the journal is a personal learning tool for the student, the structure is usually open, allowing the student to craft it in a way that works best. In it the students create a conversation between themselves and the material they're learning, and they construct a text which itself becomes an object of reflection that enables them to examine their own learning process. The openness of the journal encourages students to engage with the material not only cognitively but also affectively. It becomes an iterative process of construction in which students weave old and new ideas together, connect what they're learning to prior experience and with personal beliefs and assumptions, and through all this generate new questions that stimulate further learning.

Concept-Focused Autobiographical Writing. Apart from formal autobiographies intended for publication, autobiographical writing is typically associated with the private realm, with self-reflection directed toward greater self-understanding. But it can also be a teaching strategy. Concept-focused autobiographical writing is used to examine a topic in a course from a personal perspective and thus develop an inductive understanding of that topic. It can take many forms. Karpiak (2000) had students in an adult development course write five short chapters of their

New Directions for Adult and Continuing Education • DOI: 10.1002/ace

life story as a final paper, making their own development a focus of study. Dominicé (2000) has developed a structured seminar in which students write about their educational journey in order to examine "the way they have learned what they know" (p. 35); the concept being studied here is their own learning process. We ourselves have written about educational life histories and autobiographical learning portfolios (Rossiter and Clark, 2007). The purpose of an educational life history is to examine the experience of schooling in a person's life and is especially useful in exploring gender-based personal and structural inequities in educational institutions. The purpose of the autobiographical learning portfolio is to enable students to tell the story of their own learning in adulthood and in the process reflect on what they've learned in higher education, to understand themselves as lifelong learners, and to envision the role learning will play in the rest of their lives. In all cases of concept-focused autobiographical writing, students construct a narrative of their life experience, which must cohere in terms of a given concept and illuminate that concept. This brings together their life experience and an abstract concept to create a new narrative from which they learn.

Instructional Case Studies. This method is probably the most common mode of narrative learning and has been used extensively in professional education, particularly medicine, law, business, and public administration (Lynn, 1999; Tomey, 2003). A case is a story of professional practice, real or fictional, and it has the usual elements of story: characters, setting, and plot. It presents a problem that must be solved or an issue that must be addressed, and this is the location of the learning because the problem or issue is complex, reflecting real-world practice. The challenge to students is less to find the solution and more to figure out how to decide what to do. At one level, the narrative learning here is straightforward because students engage a problem that's in the form of a story. Their engagement is complex, however, because the story is not finished and multiple endings are possible. This open structure brings students in and makes them part of the story; they're both reader and writer. Any ending they write is by definition open and carries them deeper into the complexities of practice. They are learning to think like practitioners, which involves putting theoretical concepts in conversation with prior experience to come up with new insights and interpretations. The narrative learning here is multilayered.

Where to from Here?

In this chapter, we've laid out what we hope is a persuasive argument for narrative learning as an effective educational approach and as a valuable way to conceptualize the learning process. The question remaining is, What is the promise of this perspective? We think the concept of narrative learning opens a number of doors. For one, it should constitute a theoretical means to connect lived experience to learning at a more complex and profoundly human level. For another, it offers a different and potentially richer way to conceptualize transformational learning. We believe it can enrich adult education practice by enabling us to use stories more intentionally and effectively because narrative learning theory helps us understand how this learning works. Those are some of our ideas, at least. But, believing in narrative, we must also believe that the story is not finished, that there are other possibilities, and that other voices will enrich and expand it. We look forward to this further development.

References

Boud, D., and Walker, D. "Making the Most of Experience." *Studies in Continuing Education*, 1990, *12*(2), 61–80.

Brady, E. M., Holt, S. R., and Welt, B. "Peer Teaching in Lifelong Learning Institutes." *Educational Gerontology*, 2003, *29*(10), 851–868.

Bruner, J. *Acts of Meaning.* Cambridge, Mass.: Harvard University Press, 1990.

Clark, M. C. "Off the Beaten Path: Some Creative Approaches to Adult Learning." In S. B. Merriam (ed.), *The New Update on Adult Learning Theory.* New Directions for Adult and Continuing Education, no. 89. San Francisco: Jossey-Bass, 2001.

Cohler, B. J. "Personal Narrative and the Life Course." In P. B. Baltes and O. G. Brim, Jr. (eds.), *Life-span Development and Behavior.* New York: Academic Press, 1982.

Dominicé, P. *Learning from Our Lives: Using Educational Biographies with Adults.* San Francisco: Jossey-Bass, 2000.

Fenwick, T. J. "Expanding Conceptions of Experiential Learning: A Review of the Five Contemporary Perspectives on Cognition." Adult Education Quarterly, 2000, *50*(4), 243–272.

Fenwick, T. J. *Learning Through Experience: Troubling Orthodoxies and Intersecting Questions.* Malabar, Fla.: Krieger, 2004.

Fisher, W. R. *Human Communication as Narration: Toward a Philosophy of Reason, Value, and Action.* Columbia: University of South Carolina Press, 1987.

Freeman, M. "Rewriting the Self: Development as Moral Practice." In M. B. Tappan and M. J. Packer (eds.), *Narrative and Storytelling: Implications for Understanding Moral Development.* New Directions for Child Development, no. 54. San Francisco: Jossey-Bass, 1991.

Hansman, C. A. "Context-Based Adult Learning." In S. B. Merriam (ed.), *The New Update on Adult Learning Theory.* New Directions in Adult and Continuing Education, no. 89. San Francisco: Jossey-Bass, 2001.

Irwin, R. R. "Narrative Competence and Constructive Development Theory: A Proposal for Writing the *Bildungsroman* in the Postmodern World." *Journal of Adult Development*, 1996, *3*, 109–125.

Karpiak, I. "Writing our Life: Adult Learning and Teaching Through Autobiography." *Canadian Journal of University Continuing Education*, 2000, *26*(1), 31–50.

Kenyon, G. M., and Randall, W. L. *Restorying Our Lives: Personal Growth Through Autobiographical Reflection.* Westport, Conn.: Praeger, 1997.

Knowles, M. *The Modern Practice of Adult Education: From Pedagogy to Andragogy* (2nd ed.). New York: Cambridge Books, 1980.

Kolb, D. A. *Experiential Learning: Experience as the Source of Learning and Development.* Upper Saddle River, N.J.: Prentice Hall, 1984.

Lave, J., and Wenger, E. *Situated Learning: Legitimate Peripheral Participation.* New York: Cambridge University Press, 1991.

Linde, C. *Life Stories*. New York: Oxford University Press, 1993.

Lindeman, E. *The Meaning of Adult Education*. New York: Harvest House, 1961.

Lynn, L. E., Jr. *Teaching and Learning with Cases: A Guidebook*. New York: Chatham House, 1999.

McAdams, D. P. *Power, Intimacy, and the Life Story*. Homewood, Ill.: Dorsey Press, 1985.

Merriam, S. B., Caffarella, R. S., and Baumgartner, L. M. *Learning in Adulthood: A Comprehensive Guide* (3rd ed.). San Francisco: Jossey-Bass, 2007.

Mezirow, J. *Transformative Dimensions of Adult Learning*. San Francisco: Jossey-Bass, 1991.

Mezirow, J., and Associates (eds.). *Learning as Transformation: Critical Perspectives on a Theory in Progress*. San Francisco: Jossey-Bass, 2000.

Polkinghorne, K. E. "Narrative Knowing and the Study of Lives." In J. E. Birren and others (eds.), *Aging and Biography: Explorations in Adult Development*. New York: Springer, 1996.

Randall, W. L. "Restorying a Life: Adult Education and Transformative Learning." In J. E. Birren and others (eds.), *Aging and Biography: Explorations in Adult Development*. New York: Springer, 1996.

Rosenwald, G. C., and Ochberg, R. L. *Storied Lives*. New Haven, Conn.: Yale University Press, 1992.

Rossiter, M. *Understanding Adult Development as Narrative*. In M. C. Clark and R. S. Caffarella (eds.), New Directions for Adult and Continuing Education, no. 84. San Francisco: Jossey-Bass, 1999.

Rossiter, M., and Clark, M. C. *Narrative and the Practice of Adult Education*. Malabar, Fla.: Krieger, 2007.

Rubin, L., and Hebert, C. "Model for Active Learning: Collaborative and Peer Teaching." *College Teaching*, 1998, 46(1), 26–30.

Sarbin, T. R. "The Narrative as a Root Metaphor for Psychology." In T. R. Sarbin (ed.), *Narrative Psychology: The Storied Nature of Human Conduct*. New York: Praeger, 1986.

Sarbin, T. R. "The Narrative as the Root Metaphor for Contextualism." In S. C. Hayes, C. J. Hayes, H. W. Reese, and T. R. Sarbin, (eds.), *Varieties of Scientific Contextualism*. Reno, Nev.: Context Press, 1993.

Tomey, A. M. "Learning with Cases." *Journal of Continuing Education in Nursing*, 2003, 34(1), 34–38.

M. CAROLYN CLARK *is associate professor of adult education at Texas A&M University.*

MARSHA ROSSITER *is a member of the faculty of the College of Education and Human Services at the University of Wisconsin Oshkosh.*

7

Non-Western perspectives emphasizing community,
lifelong learning, and holistic conceptions of learning
are expanding our understanding of adult learning.

Non-Western Perspectives on Learning and Knowing

Sharan B. Merriam, Young Sek Kim

> The elder's opinion is truth. All power, all truth comes up from the roots of the family tree, the dead ancestors, to the trunk, the elders, and passes up to parents and children, the branches, leaves and flowers.
>
> —Hamminga, 2005, p. 61

As the image conveys, what counts as knowledge and truth in an African context is deeply embedded in the community and is a product of age and experience. This view is in contrast to "the western strategy of convincing with *arguments*. From the African point of view, arguments are a sign of weakness, of lack of power and vitality. A good, forceful truth does not need arguments. . . . Truth is not argued for but *felt* . . . as a force coming from the speaking human" (Hamminga, 2005, p. 61; emphasis in original).

This is but one example of how another epistemological system or worldview differs from what we in Western society are accustomed to in our understanding of adult learning. The purpose of this chapter is to introduce readers to systems of learning and knowing different from our Western perspective. Many of these systems predate Western science by thousands of years, and even today they are held by the majority of the world's peoples. We first discuss the growing awareness of non-Western perspectives. This discussion is followed by three themes characterizing adult learning in non-Western systems. We close with a discussion of how familiarity with these perspectives can extend our understanding and practice as adult educators and learners.

NEW DIRECTIONS FOR ADULT AND CONTINUING EDUCATION, no. 119, Fall 2008 © 2008 Wiley Periodicals, Inc.
Published online in Wiley InterScience (www.interscience.wiley.com) • DOI: 10.1002/ace.307

Globalization and the Non-Western World

While we were writing this chapter, the U.S. economy teetered on the brink of a recession. Stock markets in Asia, Europe, and Latin America fell and rose in sync with U.S. swings and adjustments. There can be no doubt that what happens in one part of the world today affects the rest of the world. We are in an era of globalization, of being interconnected economically, culturally, technologically, and educationally with the rest of the world. Through the global economy, technology, travel, and immigration and migration, we come into contact with people from all over the world.

This awareness of our interconnectedness has also been sharpened by our concern with how humans are affecting the health of the planet itself. As O'Sullivan (1999) points out, our science and technology has afforded us "extraordinary control. . . . We command nuclear energy. We travel into space. We know the genetic coding process. We are also in the process of destroying the carrying capacity of the earth for our species as well as the larger biotic world" (p. 180). Indeed, "it would be difficult to find an educational system in the world that was not in the midst of a navigational solution in the turbulent waters of change that globalization has brought about" (Hilgendorf, 2003, p. 72).

Many writers advocate more of a global if not a cosmic consciousness, and we can learn what this is from non-Western systems of thought. Historically, however, "we have labeled cultures as retrograde for having a larger cosmology embedded in mythic structures" and in so doing have "established western scientific thinking as superior to the thinking of other existing cultures" (O'Sullivan, 1999, p. 181). So-called Western knowledge is a relatively recent phenomenon, first spread through colonization and then through globalization. Anchored in classical Greek thought, the dominance of Western knowledge has resulted in nonattention to, if not outright dismissal of, other systems, cosmologies, and understandings about learning and knowing. Only recently have we witnessed a growing interest in learning as an embodied, spiritual, or narrative phenomenon (see the chapters in this volume), or as something structured by a wholly different worldview (Johansen and McLean, 2006; Merriam, 2007).

The terms *Western* and *non-Western* are of course problematic, beginning with the fact that setting up dichotomies in the first place is a very Western activity. Further, many indigenous peoples live in Western countries. Imperfect as it is, our use of non-Western might be thought of as a shorthand reference to systems of thought different from what we in the West have come to assume about the knowledge base of adult learning theory.

Encompassed within our use of the term *non-Western* are what are known as "indigenous" knowledge systems. Dei, Hall, and Rosenberg (2000) identify these characteristics as common to many indigenous cultures: "Seeing the individual as part of nature; respecting and reviving the wisdom of elders; giving consideration to the living, the dead, and future generations; sharing responsibility, wealth, and resources within the community; and embracing spiritual values, traditions, and practices reflecting connections to a higher order, to the culture, and to the earth" (p. 6). Our discussion of non-Western perspectives of learning and knowing thus includes indigenous knowledge systems and major philosophical and religious systems of thought. Of course, how we categorize these systems is less important than recognizing that non-Western worldviews do have something to tell us about learning and knowing.

Learning and Knowing from Non-Western Worldviews

A number of writers have compared Western and non-Western or indigenous knowledge systems. Burkhart (2004) points out that knowledge in a Western paradigm is defined by propositional statements, that is, "'that something is so'" (p. 19). Propositional knowledge is usually written, considered true, separate from the self, and permanent. Indigenous knowledge is that which we know in experience; it is "the kind of knowledge we carry with us." It is "embodied knowledge" (p. 20).

The notion that knowledge itself is fundamentally different in Western and non-Western systems leads to a difference in how knowledge is constructed, how people "learn" and the best way to instruct, that is, enable people to learn what they need to know. From reading widely, and indeed from experiencing different systems ourselves, we have selected three themes for attention: learning is communal, learning is lifelong and informal, and learning is holistic.

Learning Is Communal. In 2006, author Melissa Fay Greene published the true story of Haregewoin Teferra, an Ethiopian woman who dealt with the death of her husband and daughter by providing a refuge for children of AIDS-stricken families. Greene titled the book after an African proverb, *There Is No Me Without You.* Indeed, not only is learning a communal activity in many non-Western countries, so too is construction of one's identity. This same idea is echoed in Native American thought: "We are, therefore I am." Burkhart (2004) explains:

> In Western thought we might say that my experiences and thoughts count more than your experiences because I have them and you cannot. But if we are WE, then this constraint seems rather trivial. The hand may not have the same experiences as the foot, but this hardly matters if we understand them not as feet and hands but as this body. If it is through the body, or the people, that understanding arises, then no one part need shape this understanding [p. 26].

From this communal perspective, learning is the responsibility of all members of the community because it is through this learning that the community itself can develop.

New Directions for Adult and Continuing Education • DOI: 10.1002/ace

This notion of community and interdependence plays out in a Buddhist worldview as a form of systems theory wherein in a work setting it is important "to look at the interrelationships between ourselves, our clients, and other members of the organization. Buddhism recognizes that nothing exists in isolation; everything and everyone is the product of the interactions between other things and people" (Johansen and Gopalakrishna, 2006, p. 343).

The Hindu worldview extends this notion of community even further. In writing about the Hindu perspective on learning in the workplace, Ashok and Thimmappa (2006) point out that "individuals, organizations, society, the universe, and the cosmos are all interrelated and integrated. The development of human resources is thus viewed in terms of facilitating the individual to realize oneself and to understand the intricate relationship between the individual and his or her role in the organization, the role of the organization in the society, society in the universe, and the universe within the cosmos" (p. 329).

The individual then, does not learn for his or her own development, but for what can be contributed to the whole. In some cultures, our Western notion of personal independence and empowerment is considered immature, self-centered, and detrimental to the group (Nah, 1999). So intertwined is the individual with the community that isolation or expulsion from some communities is considered to be "worse than dying" (Hamminga, 2005, p. 59).

Related to this communal and interdependent understanding of learning is the view that one's learning must benefit the community. Human resource development (HRD) in many non-Western countries serves to develop individual employees and the corporation but is as well considered instrumental in "nation building." Today in China, national policy is promoting a learning society to address social issues that have emerged from China's exploding market economy. The goal of this lifelong learning society is the very Confucian ideal of creating a harmonious society.

In addition to learning itself being embedded in the community and for the enhancement of the community rather than the individual, in some non-Western systems one has an obligation to share what has been learned. In Islam, for example, "if there is no medical doctor to serve a community, then it is obligatory upon the community to send one or more of its members for medical training, and failure to do so will result in each member sharing the community sin" (Kamis and Muhammad, 2007, p. 28). There is an obligation to share what is learned; in many non-Western communities it is the responsibility of members to both teach and learn. In commenting on several non-Western traditions presented in his book, Reagan (2005) observed that the notion of some adults being teachers with "specialized knowledge and expertise not held by others" (p. 249) was an "alien" concept.

Learning Is Lifelong and Informal. Whispered into the ear of a newborn Muslim infant is the Muslim call to prayer; they are also the last words whispered to a dying family member. So is characterized the Muslim's lifelong journey of learning. "Muslims believe that God's knowledge is infinitely vast . . . like a drop of water in the sea; one can never complete acquiring it" (Kamis and Muhammad, 2007, pp. 34–35). This belief translates into Muslims' emphasis on learning both sacred and secular knowledge throughout their lives.

It is important to note that even though some Western scholars do promote a seamless vision of lifelong learning, one that spans the whole of a person's life, it is more commonly thought of as something for adults to engage in. Boshier (2005) has observed that in general, in the West "lifelong learning is nested in an ideology of vocationalism. Learning is for acquiring skills enabling the learner to work harder, faster and smarter and to help their employer compete in the global economy. . . . It is nested in a notion of the autonomous free-floating individual learner as consumer and mostly abdicates responsibility for the public good" (p. 375).

This more formal, market-driven version of lifelong learning is quite different from what non-Western traditions refer to when speaking of learning as lifelong. For example, from a Buddhist worldview one is consciously mindful, attending to everything in daily life throughout life, and the learning that accrues from this mindfulness is its own reward. The motivation to learn "does not rest on getting anything in particular or on being competitive with others. . . . Motivation comes out of a noble, altruistic goal for the learning, rather than a less inclusive and more selfish one of an economic or competitive nature" (Johnson, 2002, p. 110). Indeed, this mindfulness is a journey that extends through "innumerous" lives (Shih, 2007, p. 109). Likewise, Hindus see themselves on a continuous journey of learning that leads to being liberated from the cycle of rebirth and death (Thaker, 2007). Yet another perspective, Confucianism, views learning as a never-ending process toward becoming fully human (Kee, 2007).

Lifelong learning and its connection to the communal, interdependent nature of learning is particularly visible in non-Western indigenous cultures. Avoseh (2001) speaks to the interaction between being an active citizen in the community and lifelong education in traditional African society. Education "was a lifelong process that could not be separated from the rest of life's activities. Its purpose was to empower the individual to be an active member of the community" (p. 482). Indeed, lifelong learning is so embedded in the community "that anyone who fails to learn, among the Yorubas for instance, is regarded as *oku eniyan* (the living dead)" (p. 483).

What is also clear about non-Western understandings of lifelong learning is that very little of it is lodged in formal institutional settings. Lifelong learning in non-Western settings is community-based and informal. Though certainly the majority of lifelong learning is informal even in the West, the difference is that most Westerners neither recognize nor value learning that is embedded in everyday life. Most Westerners think of learning as that which occurs in a formal teacher-directed classroom with a prescribed curriculum.

New Directions for Adult and Continuing Education • DOI: 10.1002/ace

By contrast, lifelong learning in non-Western societies is structured by a community problem or issue. Resources in the form of people and materials are brought together to assess the problem and try out solutions. Such learning is "evaluated" by how effective the strategy is in addressing the problem. Fasokun, Katahoire, and Oduaran (2005) write about the informal nature of lifelong learning in Africa: informal learning "involves learning through experience under enabling conditions that facilitate the development of knowledge, skills, attitudes, aptitudes, values and interests. This is done to enhance performance, bring about change or solve practical problems" (p. 36).

The prevalence of informal learning is not to say that formal (often Western) education is not valued at all. Globalization especially has stimulated more demand for formal educational training throughout the world. However, although the West tends to conflate learning with education and formal schooling ("a tendency reflected in our concern with formal certification and degrees rather than with competence per se"), such a perspective is "far less common in non-Western traditions" (Reagan, 2005, p. 248).

Learning Is Holistic. "I think, therefore I am." Descartes's famous maxim captures the West's emphasis on learning as a cognitive process, one that takes place in the brain. Since the seventeenth century, the mind has been privileged as the site of learning and knowing. Even more recent understandings of knowing posit construction of knowledge as a process of mentally reflecting on experience. Only recently have we in adult education given serious attention to somatic knowing, that is, learning through the body, and the place of one's spirit in learning (see chapters in this volume).

If there's anything that non-Western systems of learning and knowing have in common, it's the notion that learning involves not only the mind but the body, the spirit, and the emotions. There is no separation of the mind from the rest of our being. In a discussion of the place of spirituality in Maori curriculum, for example, Fraser (2004) recounts how their holistic perspective is pictured by the Maori as their traditional meeting house. "The four walls of the house are a metaphor for the dimensions of each person. In this model, well-being (or *hauora*) comprises four components: the physical, the mental and emotional (taken as one), the social and the spiritual. . . . All four dimensions are necessary for strength and symmetry and . . . there are reciprocal influences between each one" (p. 89). Like the Maori, Native Americans see all life as interconnected, as in a circle where "everything . . . is connected to everything," and "learning must proceed in a cumulative and connected manner" (Allen, 2007, p. 51).

In non-Western traditions, learning and education are in the service of developing more than just the mind. Equally important is developing a moral person, a good person, a spiritual person, who by being part of the community uplifts the whole. In the Navajo tradition, "knowledge, learning, and life itself are *sacred, inseparable, and interwoven parts of a whole*. The quality of each determines the quality of the other" (Benally, 1997, p. 84; italics in original). In contrast, the West "separates secular and sacred knowledge and thus fragments knowledge. Consequently, some learning is forgotten soon after academic program requirements are met because it was never grounded or connected to life processes" (p. 84). Because indigenous peoples do not separate the sacred from the secular, it is not at all "personally or communally troubling" that human experiences, "especially 'religious' experiences, are not reducible to objects or logic" (Wildcat, 2001, p. 53).

Unlike the West, which privileges abstract and theoretical knowledge, non-Western traditions privilege experience in the everyday world. Learning that occurs in the experience is holistic; it has not just cognitive but physical, emotional, and sometimes spiritual dimensions, all of which are kept in balance. The Hindu tradition of Yoga, for example, employs the mind, body, and spirit in concert to work toward enlightenment. Buddhists seek a "middle way," or balance between body and mind in pursuing enlightenment. Native Americans use the medicine wheel to capture the idea of balancing the four components of a whole person (spiritual, emotional, physical, and mental): "When each aspect is developed equally, an individual is considered well-balanced and in harmony" (Hart, 1996, p. 66). The treatment of disease (dis-ease) assumes that the person is out of balance. Such notions of balance and harmony "extend to others, the family, the community, the natural and spirit worlds, to all that is living" (p. 67).

Given that learning is embedded in the context of everyday experience, active participation in everyday activities and the rites and rituals of a community are seen as conduits to learning. Learning occurs through observation of others and through practicing what is being learned. Adults are role models for younger people. In Buddhist, Hindu, Islamic, and Confucian traditions, the learner is expected to emulate teachers, sages, or more accomplished practitioners of the tradition.

Many other sources are readily recognized as mechanisms for learning in non-Western traditions. Stories, myths, and folklore define one group from another and one's place in the larger society. Rituals, symbols, music, art, theater, and even dreams and visions are also considered sources of knowledge. Ntseane (2007) notes that it is common practice in Botswana for traditional healers to rely on dreams in which spirits of the ancestors "instruct the healer on how to heal the patient and with what herbs" (p. 127).

The holistic nature of learning in non-Western traditions is of course interrelated with learning being a lifelong journey, a journey in community with others. At some level, most adult educators recognize that learning can be more than formal schooling, and knowledge can be more than abstract cognition. We turn now to how becoming acquainted with non-Western perspectives can enhance our practice.

Non-Western Perspectives and Our Practice of Adult Learning

Our exposure to non-Western perspectives of learning and knowing can influence our practice as adult educators in three ways: approaching learning holistically, valuing learning embedded in everyday life, and being responsive to learners from other cultures.

First, non-Western perspectives of learning and knowing model a holistic approach to learning, one that recognizes the interrelationship among an adult learner's body, cognition, emotion, and spirituality. Sina, a Muslim philosopher and physician in the eleventh century, for example, believed that body and emotions are closely connected; therefore a student's body can benefit when educators help students have positive emotions (Gunther, 2006). In the American Indian perspective, emotion is the foundation where we can develop a relationship between what we are learning and why we are learning it; love for people and one's land has been a primary reason for learning (Cajete, 2005). When Fraser (2004) reviewed adult learning from the perspective of the Maori, who value spirituality, she suggested that adult educators need to encourage adult learners to reflect on the meaning and purpose of life. Because the adult learner's body, cognition, emotion, and spirituality are closely interrelated, in Western society adult learners are likely to have more meaningful learning experiences if these interconnections are attended to.

Second, familiarity with non-Western perspectives of learning and knowing suggests that adult educators in Western society might place more value on learning embedded in everyday life. Because non-Westerners believe that knowledge is embedded in experiences in everyday life, they do not value what is learned in formal school settings more than what is learned in daily life. Indigenous knowledge is about what people learn in experience and deals with real problems and issues in community. Rather than emphasizing prefixed curriculum-driven learning, formal certification, and degrees, we in the West might make more visible the nonformal and informal learning that even here characterizes the majority of adult learning.

In American Indian society, for example, there is no general knowledge; each individual constructs his or her own knowledge "through patient observation and contemplation and not by question-formulation and hypothesis-testing" (Burkhart, 2004, p. 23). In addition, in Latin America, influenced by liberation theology, the grassroots community organization offers nonformal and informal learning opportunities for the poor where knowledge is transmitted in one-to-one small groups or through performance (Conceiçã and Oliveria, 2007). Western societies, which assume knowledge exists in the form of abstraction, often neglect how each individual's construction of specific knowledge in real life is valuable and how adults can teach and learn from each other to solve real-life problems outside the classroom. In practice, adult learners can be more encouraged to build their own knowledge, which can be put to use not by hypothesis testing or question formulation in the classroom but by observing and contemplating their unique experiences in real life.

Third, being familiar with non-Western perspectives of learning and knowing helps adult educators better understand how adult learners from non-Western societies act and think. With advances of technology and transportation, adult educators in Western societies are coming into contact with students who have other than Western worldviews. Many Asian learners, for example, adhere to a Confucian worldview that positions learning within the hierarchical structures of human relationships; such structures are designed to achieve a harmonious social order (Kee, 2007). Teachers thus have authority and power over students in this hierarchy. Confucianism assumes that students need to receive knowledge from teachers, without critique, and then memorize it. In Confucianism, criticizing a teacher's opinion or having opinions different from those of classical works was seen as breaking the harmonious social order; therefore, students from Confucian cultures need more guidance to think critically or engage in creative expression, both of which are valued in Western society (Yang, Zheng, and Li, 2006).

In collectivist cultures in Africa, an individual needs to take responsibility for others; individual interests are always less important than communal interests (Ntseane, 2006). For example, HIV/AIDS prevention strategies that emphasize a community problem (an ethical concern with the suffering of others) are more effective than strategies focusing on an individual health problem (the fear of death; Ntseane, 2006). Therefore, adult education practices that aim for self-actualization or personal growth would not resonate well with students from African or other collectivist cultures.

Conclusion

Our exposure to non-Western perspectives on learning and knowing broadens our understanding of adult learning and enhances our practice as educators in a global society. We hope that this chapter is just a starting point, encouraging you to look around and notice more diverse ways of learning and knowing. A more inclusive practice can enrich our lives and the lives of learners with whom we work.

References

Allen, P. G. "American Indian Indigenous Pedagogy." In S. B. Merriam (ed.), *Non-Western Perspectives on Learning and Knowing* (pp. 41–56). Malabar, Fla.: Krieger, 2007.

New Directions for Adult and Continuing Education • DOI: 10.1002/ace

Ashok, H. S., and Thimmappa, M. S. "A Hindu Worldview of Adult Learning in the Workplace." *Advances in Developing Human Resources*, 2006, *8*(3), 329–336.

Avoseh, M.B.M. "Learning to Be Active Citizens: Lessons of Traditional Africa for Lifelong Learning." *International Journal of Lifelong Education*, 2001, *20*(6), 479–486.

Benally, H. J. "The Pollen Path: The Navajo Way of Knowing." In R. P. Foehr and S. A. Schiller (eds.), *The Spiritual Side of Writing* (pp. 84–94). Portsmouth, N.H.: Boynton/Cook, 1997.

Boshier, R. "Lifelong Learning." In L. M. English (ed.), *International Encyclopedia of Adult Education* (pp. 373–378). New York: Palgrave Macmillan, 2005.

Burkhart, B. Y. "What Coyote and Thales Can Teach Us: An Outline of American Indian Epistemology." In A. Waters (ed.), *American Indian Thought* (pp.15–26). Victoria, Aus.: Blackwell, 2004.

Cajete, G. "American Indian Epistemologies." In M.J.T. Fox, S. C. Lowe, and G. S. McClellan (eds.), *Serving Native American Students* (pp. 69–78). San Francisco: Jossey-Bass, 2005.

Conceiçã, S.C.O., and Oliveria, A.M.F. "Liberation Theology and Learning in Latin America." In S. B. Merriam (ed.), *Non-Western Perspectives on Learning and Knowing* (pp. 41–56). Malabar, Fla.: Krieger, 2007.

Dei, G. J., Hall, B. L., and Rosenberg, D. G. "Introduction." In G. J. Dei, B. L. Hall, and D. G. Rosenberg (eds.), *Indigenous Knowledges in Global Contexts* (pp. 3–17). Toronto: University of Toronto Press, 2000.

Fasokun, T., Katahoire, A., and Oduaran, A. *The Psychology of Adult Learning in Africa.* Hamburg, Germany: UNESCO Institute for Education and Pearson Education, South Africa, 2005.

Fraser, D. "Secular Schools, Spirituality and Maori Values." *Journal of Moral Education,* 2004, *33*(1), 87–95.

Greene, M. F. *There Is No Me Without You: One Woman's Odyssey to Rescue Africa's Children.* New York: Bloomsbury, 2006.

Gunther, S. "Be Masters in That You Teach and Continue to Learn: Medieval Muslim Thinkers on Educational Theory." *Comparative Education Review*, 2006, *50*(3), 367–388.

Hamminga, B. "Epistemology from the African Point of View." In B. Hamminga (ed.), *Knowledge Cultures: Comparative Western and African Epistemology* (pp. 57–84). Amsterdam and New York: Rodopi, 2005.

Hart, M. A. "Sharing Circles: Utilizing Traditional Practice Methods for Teaching, Helping, and Supporting." In S. O'Meara and D. A. West (eds.), *From Our Eyes: Learning from Indigenous Peoples* (pp. 59–72). Toronto, Ont.: Garamond Press, 1996.

Hilgendorf, E. "Islamic Education: History and Tendency." *Peabody Journal of Education,* 2003, *78*(2), 63–75.

Johansen, B-C. P., and Gopalakrishna, D. "A Buddhist View of Adult Learning in the Workplace." *Advances in Developing Human Resources*, 2006, *8*(3), 337–345.

Johansen, B.-C. P., and McLean, G. W. "Worldviews of Adult Learning in the Workplace: A Core Concept in Human Resource Development." *Advances in Developing Human Resources*, 2006, *8*(3), 321–328.

Johnson, I. "The Application of Buddhist Principles to Lifelong Learning." *International Journal of Lifelong Education*, 2002, *21*(2), 99–114.

Kamis, M., and Muhammad, M. "Islam's Lifelong Learning Mandate." In S. B. Merriam (ed.), *Non-Western Perspectives on Learning and Knowing* (pp. 21–40). Malabar, Fla.: Krieger, 2007.

Kee, Y. "Adult Learning from a Confucian Way of Thinking." In S. B. Merriam (ed.), *Non-Western Perspectives on Learning and Knowing* (pp. 153–172). Malabar, Fla.: Krieger, 2007.

Merriam, S. B. (ed.). *Non-Western Perspectives on Learning and Knowing*. Malabar, Fla.: Krieger, 2007.

Nah, Y. "Can a Self-Directed Learner Be Independent, Autonomous and Interdependent?: Implications for Practice." *Adult Learning*, 1999, *11*, 18–19, 25.

Ntseane, G. "Western and Indigenous African Knowledge Systems Affecting Gender and HIV/AIDS Prevention in Botswana." In S. B. Merriam, B. C. Courtenay, and R. M. Cervero (eds.), *Global Issues and Adult Education: Perspectives from Latin America, Southern Africa, and the United States* (pp. 219–230). San Francisco: Jossey-Bass, 2006.

Ntseane, G. "African Indigenous Knowledge: The Case of Botswana." In S. B. Merriam (ed.), *Non-Western Perspectives on Learning and Knowing* (pp. 113–136). Malabar, Fla.: Krieger, 2007.

O'Sullivan, E. *Transformative Learning*. Toronto: University of Toronto Press, 1999.

Reagan, T. *Non-Western Educational Traditions: Indigenous Approaches to Educational Thought and Practice* (3rd ed.). Hillsdale, N.J.: Erlbaum, 2005.

Shih, J. "Buddhist Learning: A Process to Be Enlightened." In S. B. Merriam (ed.), *Non-Western Perspectives on Learning and Knowing* (pp. 99–112). Malabar, Fla.: Krieger, 2007.

Thaker, S. N. "Hinduism and Learning." In S. B. Merriam (ed.), *Non-Western Perspectives on Learning and Knowing* (pp. 57–74). Malabar, Fla.: Krieger, 2007.

Wildcat, D. R. "The Schizophrenic Nature of Metaphysics." In V. Deloria, Jr., and D. Wildcat, *Power and Place: Indian Education in America* (pp. 47–55). Golden, Colo.: American Indian Graduate Center and Fulcrum Resources, 2001.

Yang, B., Zheng, W., and Li, M. "Confucian View of Learning and Implications for Developing Human Resources." *Advances in Developing Human Resources*, 2006, *8*(3), 346–354.

SHARAN B. MERRIAM *is professor of adult education at the University of Georgia, Athens.*

YOUNG SEK KIM *is a Ph.D. graduate in adult education from the University of Georgia.*

8

This chapter raises the prospect of a newly emerging epistemological ecotone where adult learning has characteristics of both foundational (modern) and postmodern ways of knowing.

Troubling Adult Learning in the Present Time

Robert J. Hill

What's going on "just now"?

The French philosopher Michel Foucault asks, "What's going on just now? What's happening to us? What is this world, this period, this precise moment in which we are living?" (1982, p. 216). Answers to these questions have a profound impact on learning. The Fifth International Conference on Adult Education's (CONFINTEA V) *Agenda for the Future* (1997) focuses on "common concerns facing humanity . . . and on the vital role that adult learning has to play in enabling women and men of all ages to face [the moment's] most urgent challenges with knowledge, courage and creativity" (point 2). Article 2 of the *Hamburg Declaration on Adult Learning* (1997) states that "adult learning can shape identity and give meaning to life." What is going on just now affects learning to be, to become, to belong, and to act—principles espoused by proponents of the *Agenda for the Future*. But how, we may ask, is this learning taking place? What are its characteristics, and at what sites does it occur?

Many people in every age attempt to make sense of their "moment." This is no less true of our age, one described as postmodern by scholars. There are no agreed definitions or dates of origin of the postmodern constellation of views. It is widely diverse in its expressions and forms. But despite the lack of consensus, certain characteristics seem to define it, and certainly the antecedents to postmodernism continue to influence it.

Before probing Foucault's questions regarding the nature of this precise moment and how they relate to learning, it is important to briefly look at what has shaped our present time. We live with traces of seventeenth-century

NEW DIRECTIONS FOR ADULT AND CONTINUING EDUCATION, no. 119, Fall 2008 © 2008 Wiley Periodicals, Inc.
Published online in Wiley InterScience (www.interscience.wiley.com) • DOI: 10.1002/ace.308

Enlightenment (the Age of Reason) and eighteenth-century humanism. These are the precise moment's intellectual precursors. The preceding periods produced the belief that there is a stable, coherent, autonomous, rational, unitary self, and the idea that the world is knowable through computation, reason, and authority. Learning, it is postulated, is related to unambiguous, verifiable, and accurate knowledge of the world, with a goal toward predictability. That is, people learn through objective scientific inquiry that is neutral and value-free. What we come to "know" is called Truth—and it is universal and eternal. Data we come to know are labeled "facts." This leads to social progress, and to personal improvement. It is the "foundational" way of knowing, also described as "modernist." It holds that beliefs are justified when they are built on accepted wisdom. The current craze for "evidence-based" practice is the most recent incarnation of this positivist paradigm, a belief that the only valid knowledge is that which is generated from positive affirmation of ideas through rigorous measurement.

When applied to learning for social justice, a central thrust of adult learning today, foundationalism means that actors can rest assured they know what is "unjust," and they are authorized to produce solutions to society's ills. Quoting CONFINTEA V, Imel points out that adult learning is "'for . . . promoting democracy, justice . . . and scientific, social and economic development" (2000, para. 2). The field of adult learning is awash in these modernist notions. Examining the "signature pedagogy" of the field reveals the grip that foundational thinking has on us. One need only turn to virtually any of the *Proceedings of the Adult Education Research Conference* (www.adulterc.org/) or the premier journals of the field such as the *Adult Education Quarterly* for supporting evidence.

Social Movements: Butterflies, Mumia, Trannies, Oh My!

Social movements give the pulse of an era; therefore it is not surprising to find emerging contemporary paradigms of learning in them. Social movements introduce new values, which may eventually affect entire societies. Social movements are sites of learning, knowledge construction, meaning making, and resistance. Much has been written in adult education related to social movements and learning. Analysis of contemporary social movements offers a window into the "just now" that Foucault challenged us to probe.

Cultural critics and social theorists have recently characterized a "new" New Social Movement, called the Convergence Movement, which is sustained by convergence activism, direct action, and civil disobedience. It is a "movement of movements" that has birthed new radicalism (Klein, 2002). It is based on multiple issues of social justice and has been prompted by such factors as globalization, the shifting boundaries between public and private space, the growing income disparity in the United States (and globally), the U.S. empire, emergence of new personal identities, resistance to invisibility for the marginalized, and new information and communication technologies or ICTs (Shepard and Hayduk, 2002). It is about people's dignity and the refusal to accept being erased from the social equation. The new movement represents the volatility of social tensions building over world capitalism, U.S. militarism, and neoliberal market policies. Sites of convergence and new meaning making, where hundreds of thousands have gathered, include protests in Seattle (in 1999); Washington, D.C. (1999); Prague (2000); Quebec (2000); Göteborg (2001); Genoa (2001); Washington again (2002); and Sea Isle, Georgia (2004). Massive education and direct action training took place in and through these events.

The title of this section alludes to the linkages in disparate groups in the Convergence Movement, contributing to the fluidity of the moment. Environmentalism is symbolized by Monarch butterflies; Mumia Abu-Jamal, a former U.S. Black Panther Party member, convicted of murdering a law enforcement officer, who has become a *cause célèbre* drawing international attention with people asserting that he is a victim of a right-wing police state; and trannies, referring to transsexuals fighting for gender identity rights and freedom of gender expression. These are but a few examples of disparate constituents that make up this new movement of movements.

The Convergence Movement differs from conventional new social movements such as the lesbian and gay movement, the civil rights movement, and the feminist movement. These latter movements are deeply steeped in claims to an ultimate truth and in the stable, unitary identities of participants. That is, conventional social movements are built on the modernist notions of a collective *us* and a unitary *we*. For instance, gay men and lesbians, women, and African Americans claim to understand what it means to be members of these respective groups; the groups are essentialized. After all, without a sense of *we*, how can claims for equal rights be made? It is undisputable that organizing based on collective identity has been instrumental in social transformation.

Currently, postmodern notions contest the foundations of conventional social movements. For instance, it challenges regulation of identity, which is positioned as a subtle form of oppression (Briton, 1996). St. Pierre and Pillow (2000) remind us of the value of abandoning the desire for cohesive identity. Borrowing from the postmodern, the Convergence Movement is built on collective antioppression activism and on disrupted and reconstituted identities that in fact constitute an "anti-identity." That is, because "identity" and "essentialism" are interchangeable, the antiessentialism of the Convergence Movement that challenges identity categories is also anti-identity (Radhakrishnan, 2003). The Convergence Movement challenges the idea that race, gender, sexuality, and other demographics are fixed, permanent, and unalterable. In fact, the Convergence Movement critically mobilizes the plurality of deconstructed identities in ways that enhance democracy and social inclusion for all people. It does not produce a culture of disappearance, but rather creates a culture of visibility through difference with a goal to recognize the right of all people to be different on their own terms.

The Convergence Movement: Insights into an Emerging Paradigm

The Convergence Movement offers insights into an emerging paradigm that is actually both modern and postmodern—and neither—simultaneously. Naomi Klein, a Canadian activist, believes that we are witnessing the birth of a new radicalism (Klein, 2002) in the Convergence Movement. She reports that the emerging movement is not designed from a preset structure; rather, coherence is achieved by skillfully "surfing" the structures that are already in place. Convergence Movement actors play out life within multiple contested spheres on multiple stages.

The Convergence Movement is organized at the grass roots, has decentralized coalitions, nonhierarchical models, leaderless structures, flexible tactics, antiauthoritarianism and antinormative processes, and learning that takes place in "cells." It values broad participation, employs consensus decision making, and moves by the actions of multiple, autonomous individuals and groups. Members have mastered ICTs, and employ eye-catching visuals and sophisticated Web-based venues. It is about protests, demonstrations, occupations, vigils, and insubordinate behaviors—all acts by people that challenge postmodern notions of incredulity and suspicion of "truth." It is more about "conspiracy" than "cooperation" of players. It has borrowed practices from anarchists, radical feminists, and queers deploying behaviors that challenge mainstream conceptual and operational frames.

The Convergence Movement is dancing around and through foundational and postmodern moments in a way that might be described as peri-(post)modern. The prefix peri- is here employed to describe something that surrounds or encloses the postmodern moment. Peri-(post)modern is used as the period of transition (that is, before) the post-postmodern. Adherents unwittingly engage in the repurposing of postmodernism. Klein (2002) points out that deconstruction and abandonment of well-structured ideological arguments has not led to incoherence and fragmentation (a postmodern expectation), but rather to flexible adaptation based on convergences that are part of a common cause aimed against oppressions in all forms. When convergence members reclaim the streets, it is for all oppressed peoples as members construct them.

If postmodernism is criticism, more questions, and a series of disparate assertions of mistrust, and offering few hopeful alternatives and solutions to social problems, as some critics claim, then the peri-postmodern moment is certainly not. It generates creative solutions and owns what it is: a movement for liberation (over oppression), freedom (over marginalization), and simplicity (over complicity). The peri-postmodern condition seen in the

New Directions for Adult and Continuing Education • DOI: 10.1002/ace

Convergence Movement disturbs the dichotomy of foundationalism-postmodernism because it recognizes that within the latter are to be found irrationality and fragmentation, and within the former emancipation to be realized. The peri-postmodern celebrates the death of identity and its resurrection as a contested space where essentialist notions are assaulted.

The Convergence Movement challenges Cole and Hill's claim that "postmodernism refutes the idea of any common interest between oppressed groups . . . disallowing any action in common" (1999, p. 12). It is typical for movement members to find direct links, and pursue common action, between and among sex workers' rights, radical environmentalism, revolutionary notions of democracy, direct rebellious action for HIV/AIDS funding, abortion rights; against the racist prison industrial complex, antinuclear activism, the ethical treatment of animals, activism against genetically modified organisms (GMOs); support for Palestinians living under Israeli apartheid, radical sexual politics, the urban (green guerrilla) gardening movement, and antiglobalization and antineoliberalism (against Starbucks, Wal-Mart, Coke, and McDonalds).

It includes spontaneous episodes of culture jamming—a form of critical adult education practice (Sandlin, 2007) that resists the hegemony of the homogeneous popular culture of our times. Culture jamming fuses adult education's foundational ties to certainty in learning for social justice with postmodernism's incredulity to truth. Learning is waged through insurrectionary tactics, exploiting ICTs such as the Internet, and employing hacktivism (breaking into computers), détournement (the reuse of elements of popular media to generate a new work with a message that challenges the original), subvertisements (subversive advertisement), and the blogosphere (computer blogs and their interconnections).

Supporting the notion that the present moment has spawned a new paradigm, we can look to contemporary queer discourse where a further example of the peri-postmodern is found. Queer discourse points to an alternative way to be in the world, with a new frame to analyze and conceptualize our present moment. It affirms a new identity (for example, queer, which is *not* lesbian or gay), while refusing normative constructions of sexuality. Paradoxically it constructs an essential nonessential self.

The peri-postmodern emerges on other fronts as well, raising the question, "Are we approaching a post Post period?" For instance, in addition to rejection (deregulation) of identities such as gay or lesbian, there is currently a clear generational shift toward a postracial and postethnic moment. In the National Public Radio segment "Post-Racial America" (2003), the author avers that, "when asked about their race, many young people are more likely to say something like Blaxican, Mexipino, Chino-latino, than one of the sixty-three color-coded Census categories." Also exemplary is the exhibit "Remix: New Modernities in a Post-Indian World," at the internationally renowned Heard Museum for the cultural heritage of Native American peoples in Phoenix, which "explores what it means to be of mixed heritage with strong ties—and sometimes absent ties—to Native communities" ("Remix," 2007) It is about being the non-Indian Indian and the Indian non-Indian simultaneously.

In ecology, an ecotone is the transition region between two adjacent ecological communities; it has shared characteristics of both and of neither, evidenced by emergent new properties. Odum (1966), the founder of modern ecology, offers that "an ecotone is a . . . junction zone or tension belt . . . [with] the tendency for increased variety and density [of life] . . . known as the 'edge effect'" (p. 278). The peri-(post)modern illustrates an epistemological ecotone. The new postidentity self, not unlike the Convergence Movement already described, is a hybrid location, a place that creates "new . . . forms within [a] contact zone" (Ashcroft, Griffiths, and Tiffin, 2003, p. 118). What is intriguing is that these postidentities are constructed by "insiders" rather than by members of the dominant group—insiders who trouble notions of what it means to be a gay, a black or brown person, a woman or a man. Equally interesting is the fact that identity-driven academic discourse largely fails to embrace the emerging postidentity movement, and in fact actively resists it. The "old" (foundational) and the "new" (postmodern) are in a state of interdependent mutuality; this tension belt constitutes a "third space" (Bhabha, 1995).

Meaning Making in the Epistemological Ecotone

Meaning making with and in the epistemological ecotone is linked to learning in numerous ways. A substantial number of young people claim they acquire knowledge through the politics of humor (for example, Jon Stewart's "news" show or "Saturday Night Live"). Other venues include popular education and learning for emancipation in grassroots organizations. Radical citizenship education and radical democracy do not simply ask for rights on the basis of diversity but actually foster continuous proliferation of new forms of difference, of "new voices, new communities, and new identities, as part of an ongoing process of democratization" (Sandilands, 1993, para. 6). There is a powerful learning dimension to critical consumption activism (Flowers, 2007), and arts-based inquiry (street theater, dance, song, and larger-than-life puppetry).

Living in the ecotone demands that learners make meaning in the context of "what if" questions (Hill, 2004, p. 88), important questions first raised by St. Pierre, Hill, and Lewis (2003). What if one person's liberation is another's condemnation? What if empathy for marginalized and oppressed people is nothing more than forced intimacy that, in the end, appropriates the Other and erases difference? What if the learning associated with advocacy work is more about the cultural capital, privilege, and elitism of the one facilitating justice work than getting out of the way of the dreams, desires, pleasures, joys, and angers of the "rescued"? What if conflict and confrontation are the only means within the current cultural framework

New Directions for Adult and Continuing Education • DOI: 10.1002/ace

where difference can be constantly reestablished? What if we adult educators are naïve when we think our liberal projects can liberate without revolutionary dismantling of a system that is beyond band-aids?

If being postmodern means falling into relativism, learning associated with the peri-(post)modern is not. It operates from a moral and ethical framework. If the postmodern ends in more questions than solutions to life's problems, learning in the Convergence Movement does not. Foundational values in the ecotone include purpose, creation, and interpretation, within a radical critique. The Convergence Movement, as in postmodernism, plays with notions of a collective *we*. It offers new possibilities of conduct toward and treatment of difference. If postmodernism is soulless and hopeless and the place where an entire generation of adherents have elected to drown (Berman, 1982), this surely is not.

No Conclusion, But a Few Afterthoughts

"All conclusions are genuinely provisional and therefore inconclusive" (Derrida, 1997, p. xiii). To conclude is to preclude different interpretations and to forestall the opening of new possibilities. With this in mind, I cannot write a conclusion. But the question, "How do we proceed?" remains germane. These afterthoughts might permit conversation to move forward.

Learning is the process of making sense of experiences. It is a lifelong adventure. In fact, Lindeman (1926) promoted the idea that learning is "not merely preparation for an unknown kind of future living. . . . The whole of life is learning" (p. 5). Knowles (1980) further developed this concept. It is critical to understand that learning, based in experience, is inextricably linked to the precise moment in which the learner finds herself or himself, which today is heavily influenced by postmodern notions. Lyotard (1979/1984) describes the postmodern condition as increasingly skeptical toward universal truths, which are known as metanarratives (also called grand narratives or master narratives). Metanarratives are comprehensive ways to order and explain knowledge and experience. Metanarratives proliferate in adult education. For example, Zemke and Zemke (1984) make the claim that there are "30 Things We Know for Sure about Adult Learning," and Delahoussaye and Zemke (2001) report that there are "10 Things We Know for Sure About Learning Online." The "facts" found in these and other foundational texts on adult learning are troubled in the present moment's tension belt.

Adult learning is often situated as the quest for truth, authenticity, and what is right. These tenets have major implications for learning because they lead to the belief in an ultimate basis for knowledge. This way of knowing acts to justify and explain our social structures and institutions (Klages, 2007, para. 28) and the learning that takes place within them. Postmodern critique introduces a deep skepticism about authentic meanings in our present time (St. Pierre and Pillow, 2000). Because postmodernism argues for the impossibility of an ultimate basis for knowledge, it poses dilemmas for adult education's search for ultimate truths.

Postmodern notions that lay claim to ambiguity and the impossibility of truth and authenticity have only slowly infiltrated the dominant discourses in adult education. Where they have encroached, they have been both demonized and valorized. For example, Ellsworth's claim (1997) that postmodernism frees learning related to race, gender, ethnicity, and sexuality from the tyranny of leftist grand narratives can be used to illustrate postmodernism's value to the field. On the other hand, Edwards and Usher (2001) point out, "The location of adult education within a postmodern landscape has been, and continues to be, a troubled one" (p. 275).

Although some adult educators have critiqued the traces from the Enlightenment (for example, decentering the dichotomies of teacher-learner, theory-practice, and researcher-researched), few have explored the intersection of adult learning and social justice from a contemporary postmodern frame. To do so is to ask, "What does it mean to trouble notions like oppression and marginalization?" Hemphill (2001), commenting on our precise moment, offers that the "complex cultural and technological changes that are now underway will unavoidably have major effects on how we conceive of knowledge—its construction, conceptualization, storage, transmission, and social function" (p. 27). He warns that "adult education is too important an enterprise to be left to ossify in a decaying [foundational] paradigm" (p. 27). In the Convergence Movement, influenced by peri-(post)modernism, we find evidences that adult learning, caught in an epistemological ecotone, is rupturing from the rigid conventional modernist patterns of which Hemphill warns us.

Appignanesi and Garratt (1995) ask, "Can we imagine how postmodernism might end? End in what? It doesn't have a specifiable beginning . . . but is a continued enmeshment in modernity" (p. 172). They remind the reader that shortly before his death in 1984, Foucault "called for a re-thinking of the Enlightenment. The Grand Narrative philosophers who seemed off the agenda are suddenly back on again" (p. 173). Does the learning in epistemological ecotone rekindle metanarratives of social justice and human rights, perhaps as Foucault foresaw?

The Convergence Movement points to a precise moment that positions traditional (foundational) ways and postmodernism as having the same referent; that is, they deal with the same social situation and offer insights into human agency. It is a moment of contradiction, complexity, and hybridity. Perhaps the precise moment merely reflects what the Marxist humanist Marshall Berman (1982) has suggested: the appearance of another incarnation of the fluid nature of the experience of modernity. After all, things "modern" are relative. The term appears to have been first applied by Abbot Suger nine hundred years ago. He described the new Middle Age monastery of St. Denis as *opus modernum*, meaning a work that was "just now" (Appignanesi and Garratt, 1995). It was a clear disruption of the then-contemporary

Romanesque style of architecture. However, the just now never stands still; it is always in motion. Thus, learning in the postmodern is not simply a break from the past but rather comprises the past's elements in motion. The peri-postmodern moment is all of the contradiction that surrounds the new just now. It vexes us with the question, "Is it a harbinger of a post Postmodern moment" ushering in something yet to be described and understood?

References

Agenda for the Future. CONFINTEA V, 1997. Retrieved January 23, 2008, from www.unesco.org/education/uie/confintea/agendeng.htm.

Appignanesi, R., and Garratt, C. *Introducing Postmodernism*. New York: Totem Books, 1995.

Ashcroft, B., Griffiths, G., and Tiffin, H. *Post-Colonial Studies: The Key Concepts*. London: Routledge, 2003.

Berman, M. *All That Is Solid Melts into Air: The Experience of Modernity*. London: Verso, 1982.

Bhabha, H. K. "Cultural Diversity and Cultural Differences." In B. Ashcroft, G. Griffiths, and H. Tiffin (eds.), *The Post-Colonial Studies Reader*. London: Routledge, 1995.

Briton, D. *The Modern Practice of Adult Education: A Postmodern Critique*. Albany: State University of New York Press, 1996.

Cole, M., and Hill, D. "Resistance Postmodernism and the Ordeal of the Undecidable: A Marxist Critique." British Educational Research Association Annual Conference, Sept. 2–5, 1999.

Delahoussaye, M., and Zemke, R. "10 Things We Know for Sure About Learning Online." *Training*, 2001, *38*(9), 48–59.

Derrida, J. *Of Grammatology* (G. C. Spivak, trans.). Baltimore, Md.: Johns Hopkins University Press, 1997.

Edwards, R., and Usher, R. "Lifelong Learning: A Postmodern Condition of Education?" *Adult Education Quarterly*, 2001, *51*(4), 273–287.

Ellsworth, E. *Teaching Positions: Difference, Pedagogy, and the Power of Address*. New York: Teachers College Press, 1997.

Flowers, R. "Critical Consumption Activism, Popular Education and Emancipatory Civil Society." Proceedings of the Conference on Cosmopolitan Civil Societies, University of Technology, Sydney (Australia), pp. 32–33, Oct. 4–5, 2007. Retrieved Feb. 16, 2008, from www.shopfront.uts.edu.au/news/ccsconferenceprogramforwebsite1.pdf.

Foucault, M. "The Subject and Power." In H. L. Dreyfus and P. Rabinow (eds.), *Michel Foucault: Beyond Structuralism and Hermeneutics*. Chicago: University of Chicago Press, 1982.

Hamburg Declaration on Adult Learning, 1997. Retrieved Jan. 23, 2008, from www.unesco.org/education/uie/confintea/declaeng.htm.

Hemphill, D. F. "Incorporating Postmodernist Perspectives into Adult Education." In V. Sheared and P. A. Sissel (eds.), *Making Space: Merging Theory and Practice in Adult Education*. Westport, Conn.: Bergin and Garvey, 2001.

Hill, R. J. "Activism as Practice: Some Queer Considerations." In R. St. Clair and J. A. Sandlin (eds.), *Promoting Critical Practice in Adult Education*. New Directions for Adult and Continuing Education, no. 102. San Francisco: Jossey-Bass, 2004.

Imel, S. "International Perspectives on Adult Education." ERIC *Trends and Issues Alert no. 14*, 2000. Retrieved Apr. 10, 2008, from www.calpro-online.org/eric/docs/tia00082.pdf.

Klages, M. *Literary Theory: A Guide for the Perplexed*. New York: Continuum Press, 2007.

Klein, N. "The Vision Thing: Were the DC and Seattle Protests Unfocused, or Are Critics Missing the Point?" In B. Shepard and R. Hayduk (eds.), *From ACT UP to the WTO:*

Urban Protest and Community Building in the Era of Globalization. New York: Verso, 2002.

Knowles, M. S. *The Modern Practice of Adult Education: From Pedagogy to Andragogy* (2nd ed.). New York: Cambridge Books, 1980.

Lindeman, E. *The Meaning of Adult Education.* New York: New Republic, 1926.

Lyotard, J.-F. *The Post Modern Condition: A Report on Knowledge* (G. Bennington and B. Massumi, trans.). Theory and History of Literature, Vol. 10. Minneapolis: University of Minnesota Press, 1984. (Originally published in 1979.)

Odum, E. P. *Fundamentals of Ecology.* Philadelphia: Saunders, 1966.

"Post-Racial America." 2003. Retrieved Mar. 9, 2008, from www.theconnection.org/shows/2003/07/20030703_b_main.asp.

Radhakrishnan, R. *Theory in an Uneven World.* Malden, Mass.: Blackwell, 2003.

"Remix: New Modernities in a Post-Indian World." 2007. Retrieved Mar. 9, 2008, from www.heard.org/NETCOMMUNITY/Page.aspx?&pid=610&srcid=363.

Sandilands, K. "Radical Democracy: _A Contested/ing Terrain." *Synthesis/Regeneration,* 1993, 5. Retrieved Mar. 9, 2008, from www.greens.org/s-r/05/05–13.html.

Sandlin, J. "Popular Culture, Cultural Resistance, and Anticonsumption Activism: An Exploration of Culture Jamming as Critical Adult Education." In E. J. Tisdell and P. M. Thompson (eds.), *Popular Culture and Entertainment Media in Adult Education.* New Directions for Adult and Continuing Education, no. 115. San Francisco: Jossey-Bass, 2007.

Shepard, B., and Hayduk, R. (eds.). *From ACT UP to the WTO: Urban Protest and Community Building in the Era of Globalization.* New York: Verso, 2002.

St. Pierre, E. A., Hill, R. J., and Lewis, J. "Advocacy Research: Tensions Between Critical and Postmodern Theories and Methods in Speaking for Others." Panel and workshop presented at the 16th Annual Conference on Interdisciplinary Qualitative Studies (QUIG), Contact Zones: Advocacy Research on a Global Platform, Athens, Georgia, Jan. 4–6, 2003.

St. Pierre, E. A., and Pillow, W. (eds.). *Working the Ruins: Feminist Poststructuralist Theory and Methods in Education.* New York: Routledge, 2000.

Zemke, R., and Zemke, S. "30 Things We Know for Sure About Adult Learning." *Innovation Abstracts,* 1984, 6(8). Retrieved Feb. 21, 2008, from http://honolulu.hawaii.edu/intranet/committees/FacDevCom/guidebk/teachtip/adults-3.htm.

ROBERT J. HILL *is an associate professor of adult education at the University of Georgia whose interests include learning in social movements.*

9

Drawing from previous chapters in this volume, this final chapter proposes that adult learning theory is attending more to the various contexts where learning takes place and to its multidimensional nature.

Adult Learning Theory for the Twenty-First Century

Sharan B. Merriam

The one thing that all of us educators of adults have in common, regardless of our work setting or learner population, is that facilitating learning is at the heart of our practice. Whether we are assisting adults in preparing for the GED, coaching executives in a Fortune 500 company, or demonstrating a new agricultural technique in a developing country, the more we know about how adults learn the better we are able to structure learning activities that resonate with those adult learners with whom we work. This third update volume offers readers glimpses into some of the recent thinking and research in adult learning. It is not meant to be a comprehensive guide to adult learning theory, but rather a snapshot as to recent developments in understanding and theorizing adult learning.

We are in a much different place today with regard to adult learning theory than even when the second update was published in 2001. Embodied learning, spirituality, and narrative learning were topics only briefly touched on in the 2001 edition. This third update has separate chapters on embodied learning, spirituality and learning, and narrative learning. In addition to these new chapters, there are chapters on the latest constructions of workplace learning, non-Western perspectives on learning, the most recent developments in postmodernism, and what neuroscience has to tell us about the brain and learning.

The only constant across three updates is a chapter in each one on transformational learning (TL). But there are important differences in emphasis across the three chapters, as reflects major developments in this theory.

In 1993, the chapter on TL was mostly a description of theory as particularly laid out by Mezirow; in 2001 there was much more of an empirical research base to draw from; and in this most recent update, not only has the empirical work continued but diverse theoretical perspectives have also emerged.

What this review of the updates over just the last fifteen years has to tell us is that adult learning theory is a dynamic area of research and theory building. Adult learning is a complex phenomenon that can never be reduced to a single, simple explanation. Rather, I think what we have is an ever-changing mosaic where old pieces are rearranged and new pieces are added. So what we might conclude about adult learning today will most likely be out of date by the time this volume is a year old.

However, on the basis of the chapters in this volume, I think some observations can be advanced about what is characterizing adult learning theory at the moment, and where we seem to be heading. Two such observations are that there is increased attention to the various contexts where learning takes place, and learning is a multidimensional phenomenon, not just a cognitive activity.

Increased Attention to the Learning Context

Beginning with behaviorist research in the early decades of the twentieth century, adult learning theory in North America has focused on the individual learner, how that learner processes information, and how learning enables the individual to become more empowered and independent. Andragogy and self-directed learning are about the individual adult learner, as has been much of Mezirow's conceptualization of transformational learning. It wasn't until the 1980s that the field began to attend to the context in which learning takes place. This awareness was fostered by the infusion of situated cognition theory, feminist theory, critical social theory, and postmodern theory.

Today the historical, sociocultural context of adult learning is recognized as a key component in understanding the nature of adult learning. In her chapter on workplace learning, Fenwick makes this point in observing that workplace learning is "not just human change but interconnections of humans and their actions with rules, tools and texts, cultural, and material environments." Some of the new perspectives consider learning as part of the system's cultural and historical norms. An emerging line of research in workplace learning is literally context-based, as researchers consider how physical space and spatiality encourages or inhibits learning.

Two other chapters in particular focus on the context in which learning takes place. In his discussion of new developments in postmodern thinking, Hill introduces us to the new New Social Movement called the Convergence Movement, where learning is meaning making through such contexts as popular education, radical citizenship education, and critical consumption activism. The chapter on non-Western perspectives of learning and knowing juxtaposes the Western context of learning from an individual perspective to the communal orientation of many non-Western epistemologies. Just in these three chapters, the workplace, social movements, and non-Western cultures are forms of context that expand our thinking beyond the individual learner.

In the other chapters of this update, context is quite present in considering a particular form of learning. For example, in Tisdell's chapter on spirituality and learning, she notes that spiritual development often involves "reclaiming" one's cultural heritage. In the chapter on transformative learning, Taylor reviews several formulations that are more context-sensitive than Mezirow's theory, including Freire's social-emancipatory view, a cultural-spiritual view, and a planetary orientation that "recognizes the interconnectedness among universe, planet, natural environment, human community, and personal world." Chapters on the brain, narrative learning, and embodied learning also recognize that such learning is firmly embedded in the lived experiences of learners in the world.

Thus the spotlight has definitely shifted from understanding adult learning from the individual learner's perspective to the learner *in context*. I am conceiving of *context* as a broad concept referring to where the learner is situated concretely (as in the workplace) or socioculturally (as in working-class America, Confucian society, and so on). This linking of the individual's learning process to his or her context makes for a richer, more holistic understanding of learning in adulthood.

Recognition That Learning Is a Multidimensional Phenomenon

For a good part of the twentieth century, adult learning was understood as a cognitive process, one in which the mind took in facts and information, converting it all to knowledge, which then could be observed as subsequent behavior change. Although there is still research going on in memory and information processing, especially as a function of age, currently learning is construed as a much broader activity involving the body, the emotions, and the spirit as well as the mind. Even reviewing the technical aspects of how the brain functions in learning, Taylor and Lamoreaux in their chapter on the brain point out that for the brain to make meaningful connections, learning needs to be tied to physical, embodied experience: "The brain's physical responses to the sensory data are recorded—literally, embodied—as experience, hence accessible to reconstruction as memory; without such physical responses, there is no basis for constructing meaning." The brain is, after all, a part of one's body. Yet another connection can be made between the mental and the physical. Recent studies using imaging techniques to study brain functioning, according to Ed Taylor's chapter on transformative learning theory, have found that the structure of the brain itself changes during the learning process. The "neurobiological" approach to transformative learning suggests that such learning "is strengthened by emotive, sensory, and kinesthetic experiences."

The multidimensional nature of learning is often construed as taking a more holistic approach to learning. Freiler's chapter on learning through the body most prominently makes the case that learning is a holistic endeavor. From the Moken sea gypsies who "felt" the December 2004 tsunami coming on and so fled to high land, to miners and athletes who are acutely conscious of embodied space, to using embodied learning activities in the classroom, the body has become more visible as a source of knowledge and site for learning. But it is not that the body is merely a vehicle for learning; it is what the body *feels*, the affective dimension of learning, that combines with the intellect in significant learning.

In addition to the mind-body connection resurfacing in the adult learning literature, spirituality and its relationship to adult learning and adult education has emerged as a prominent stream of writing and research in the last ten years. We can only speculate why spirituality is now receiving attention; perhaps we turn to it to guide and inspire us in a fast-paced, uncertain world; or perhaps because learning is now seen as more multidimensional, spirituality is "safe" to discuss. Tisdell explores many facets of this attention to spirituality, pointing out that spirituality in adult education can be found in the practice of social justice educators, in the workplace, and in the experiences of individual learners.

Yet another facet of this multidimensional approach to adult learning is the emergence of narrative learning as a way to theorize learning. Clark and Rossiter's chapter on this topic makes the observation that we "story" our lives to give meaning to our experiences. Learning can be construed as meaning making; therefore narrative is a form of learning. We learn through stories of others, but also "when we're learning something, what we're essentially doing is trying to make sense of it, discern its internal logic, and figure out how it's related to what we know already." We create a narrative, a story, about what we've learned. Narratives exist on many levels: the individual, family, society, the workplace, and so on. One of postmodernism's tasks, according to Hill, is to take on and critique some of the "metanarratives" of adult learning. Metanarratives are "comprehensive ways to order and explain knowledge and experience"; they are stories about what we believe to be true.

Storying our experiences and recognizing that the body and the spirit are important components in learning are quite commonplace in non-Western epistemological systems. Globalization and communications technology have resulted in adult educators in the West becoming more aware of diverse worldviews and epistemologies regarding learning and knowing. Interaction with people from all over the world has promoted an awareness of different perspectives on learning, teaching, and what counts as knowledge. These perspectives are now informing our understanding of learning and how best to promote learning.   Kim and I explore some of these perspectives in our chapter on non-Western systems of thought. We found that non-Western systems eschew mind-body, emotion-reason, and individual-group dichotomies and see learning as holistic, lifelong, and community-based.

Whether it be from non-Western epistemological systems or from our own Western perspective, it appears that adult learning research and theory building are expanding to include more than just an individual, cognitive understanding of learning. The mind, body, spirit, emotions, and society are not themselves simply sites of learning; learning occurs in their intersections with each other.

Fostering Adult Learning

Recognition that adult learning is more than cognitive processing, that it is a multidimensional phenomenon, and that it takes place in various contexts has not only enhanced our understanding of *how* adults learn but expanded our thinking as to which instructional strategies might be employed to foster adult learning. Each chapter in this update is anchored in practice in terms of what each dimension of adult learning "looks like" in the real world, but also what strategies we might make use of in promoting such learning. Not surprisingly, there is a fair amount of overlap across the chapters.

When adult learning is construed as meaning making or knowledge construction, as all the authors maintain, then several strategies are particularly recommended. Encouraging reflection and dialogue, whether with the self, another, or a group, enables learning to take place. However, learning to reflect—especially in a critical manner—is itself a developmental process that needs to be fostered in adult learning settings. Critical reflection is essential for transformative learning, for engaging in the new New Social Movements, for developing brain capacity, and for confronting power and politics in workplace learning.

Connecting new learning with learners' previous experience is a long-standing strategy promoted by adult educators since Lindeman and Knowles. Recent research in several areas has confirmed the importance of processing new information or experience with prior experiences. Brain-based research has documented that "when storing new sensory input, the brain 'looks for' connections to earlier information" (Chapter Five). These connections are our "learnings"; with no meaningful links to prior experience, little if anything is retained. In narrative learning, stories can both draw us into an experience from which we can learn and enable us to make meaning of an experience. Embodied learning requires that we attend to the body in our experiences. Tisdell's research on spirituality (Chapter Three) suggests that significant spiritual experiences from which we learn are those related to life experiences where we "see the extraordinary in the ordinary business of life."

Finally, in addition to connecting with the learner's life experiences and promoting reflection and dialogue, all the authors recommend expanding our repertoire of instruction to include creative and artistic modes of inquiry. Non-Western and indigenous knowledge systems have always turned to stories, folklore, myths, symbols, music, dance, and even dreams as sources of knowledge. With the growing understanding that adult learning is a multidimensional and holistic phenomenon, we are beginning to recognize the value of incorporating more creative modes of inquiry into our practice.

What then of adult learning theory for the twenty-first century? The authors of chapters in this volume seem to be saying very similar things: that there is an ever-expanding understanding of what adult learning is and can be. We need only attend to our own mind, body, spirit, and emotions and the sociocultural and material contexts in which we ourselves learn to recognize the potential of this expanded vision for our adult learners.

SHARAN B. MERRIAM is professor of adult education at the University of Georgia, Athens.

New Directions for Adult and Continuing Education • DOI: 10.1002/ace

INDEX

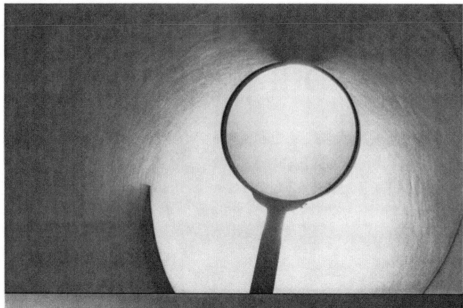